Clinical Quantitative Methods

CLINICAL QUANTITATIVE METHODS

RICHARD W. J. NEUFELD, PH.D.
Associate Professor of Psychology and
Coordinator, Doctoral-Training Program
in Clinical and Experimental Psychopathology
University of Western Ontario
London, Ontario, Canada

Grune & Stratton
A Subsidiary of Harcourt Brace Jovanovich, Publishers
New York • San Francisco • London

WILLIAM MADISON RANDALL LIBRARY UNC AT WILMINGTON

Library of Congress Cataloging in Publication Data

Neufeld, Richard W   J
   Clinical quantitative methods.

   Includes bibliographies and index.
   1. Psychiatric research.   2.   Psychometrics.
I.   Title.   [DNLM: 1.   Statistics.   HA29 N482c]
RC337.N47   616.8'9'00182   77-13710
ISBN 0-8089-1035-3

© 1977 by Grune & Stratton, Inc.
All rights reserved. No part of this publication
may be reproduced or transmitted in any form or
by any means, electronic or mechanical, including
photocopy, recording, or any information storage
and retrieval system, without permission in
writing from the publisher.

Grune & Stratton, Inc.
111 Fifth Avenue
New York, New York 10003

Distributed in the United Kingdom by
Academic Press, Inc. (London) Ltd.
24/28 Oval Road, London NW1

Library of Congress Catalog Number 77-13710
International Standard Book Number 0-8089-1035-3

Printed in the United States of America

RC 337
.N47

To my mother and father

181858

Contents

Preface

This book is written for those engaged in or studying some branch of clinical activity. The contents are oriented toward the disciplines of clinical psychology and psychiatry, with most of the illustrations taken from those fields; however, it should be a relatively easy matter to extrapolate from there to other clinical disciplines. The book is written from the perspective of a clinician rather than a statistician. Perhaps a nonstatistician has little business writing a book on quantitative methods; but a clinician who believes that his discipline should be a rational science and that the experimental metod should be extended as far as possible into clinical endeavors, does have business writing a book with the aim of promoting this approach among other clinicians. Those wishing a mathematically sophistocated presentation of the methods presented within these pages may consult the numerous advanced statistical references cited throughout the book.

One audience likely to benefit from the book are students needing a supplement to their current knowledge of quantititative methods which will help them bridge the gap between analytical techniques and clinical practice and research. Another audience apt to find the book useful are professional clinicians or teachers who wish to gain a better understanding of reports in the literature which use advanced quantitative methods; or, who wish to update their knowledge of quantitative methods so as to apply them in their own practice or research. This book should also be of value to the clinician who already uses advanced methods but does so more or less mechanically through packaged computer programs and "cookbook" formulas. This material should help such a user acquire more information from his data through a better knowledge of when to apply a given method and what the results mean afterwards.

There is little emphasis on computer programming. With a number of excellent treatments of the subject and so many packaged programs already available, another discourse by someone whose expertise is not in that area would be otiose. Furthermore, the barrier preventing the clinician from using many quantitative methods is not one of computational labor—most computer programs can simply be "called up," or a consultant can be hired to write a special one. Rather, the barrier is typically a lack of understanding of the goals and rationale of available methods.

Selection of the material was based on two criteria. The first was that the methods have a rather immediate application to a large number of common clinical problems. Put another way, the methods were to have "face validity" regarding their relevance to clinical endeavors. The second criterion was that they not already be widely known among clinicians. The selection of material on this basis was necessarily a matter of subjective judgment, but it is important to explicate the criteria on which the subjective judgments—fallible though they be—were made. Using these criteria, factor analysis has not been given a formal treatment since it is already familiar to most clinicians and many excellent volumes on the subject are currently available. The use of the Repertory Grid has not been included since it is largely a property of those operating within a specific theoretical framework (Kelly's Personal Construct Theory). Readers interested in multivariate analysis of variance can get a start on the subject by reading the section on discriminant-function analysis in Chapter 8 as it includes the usual significance test of the one-way multivariate analysis of variance.

By way of preparation in statistics, it is assumed that the reader has had an introductory course including analysis of variance. This topic is especially important because of the many analogies drawn to it throughout the book. The conventional Fisherian approach, rather than the more recent regression approach, has been emphasized because the former's greater familiarity to most students.

A debt of gratitude is owed to Park Davidson and Charles Costello for their encouragement of the idea for the book during its early phases. I would like to acknowledge Douglas Jackson and Ian Spence for their helpful consultation during its writing. I also owe gratitude to my wife, Marilyn, for her proofreading and comments on writing style in several of the early chapters.

RICHARD W. J. NEUFELD

Clinical Quantitative Methods

1

Introduction

**RELATIONS BETWEEN CLINICAL ENDEAVORS AND
QUANTITATIVE METHODS**

The clinician is both a decision maker and problem solver. The majority of clinical activities with individual patients, whether they are concerned with classification, selection of a treatment of choice, monitoring treatment effectiveness, or estimating prognosis, involve some form of decision making or problem solving. The majority of clinical activities dealing with treatment programs can also be described as essentially decision making and problem solving. The decision-making process involves acquiring as much relevant information as is possible, and applying it to the problem at hand to determine the best estimate of the outcomes from alternative cources of action. A specific course of action is then selected according to these estimated outcomes so that maximum benefits will accrue to the entity of concern. The entity may be a specific patient; a group of patients involved in a treatment program; or, in some cases, the treatment institution or facility.

A critical component to effective decision making is that of maximizing the information available in the problem-relevant data. Vital information may be lost if the critical aspects of the data are not detected or if less than the total amount of available information is extracted. The best course of action for a patient or treatment program is risked if, (a), the clinician cannot condense the relevant

1

data into a parsimonious set of information which can then be entered into the decision-making operation, or (b), if the means of condensing the data yields less than all of the relevant information available from the data pool. Indeed, a great deal of data containing problem-relevant information lies dormant in such sources as hospital files because the clinician is unaware of methods for extracting it. Information can in effect be "created" as the clinician becomes aware of extant methods for tapping it.

One of the barriers to maximum data utilization in the clinical setting is a lack of awareness of available analytical methods. Another barrier is the apparent complexity of the methods in presentations designed for more mathematically sophisticated audiences. Given a lack of understanding of the methods, their relevance to clinical problems will probably not be appreciated, leaving little motivation to pursue them.

The intention in this book is to increase awareness of available methods for analyzing data which are relevant to clinical endeavors and to present the rationale and basic computations of the methods. Examples are taken from published data and from contrived data of hypothetical problems in order to illustrate the clinical relevance of the individual procedures.

Although the focus is on quantitative methods, the clinician's knowledge of his subject matter is a vital agent in maximizing problem-relevant information. The results from even the most elegant analytical method will be of limited value if the user has little expertise in the substantive domain in which it is being applied. On the other hand, a clinician who is most knowledgeable in clinical subject matter will be curtailed in his information-gathering endeavors if he is tied to suboptimal analytical methods. The strategic combination is one where the clinician is well versed in clinical subject matter and has at the same time maximized his analytical options.

An approach frequently taken in the past has been to assign the problems of analyzing clinical data to someone specializing in quantitative methods. Often this person is a nonclinician. This approach is better than one of ignoring analytical alternatives altogether, but it has several disadvantages: The analysis consultant may not be available when needed, or he often enters the picture only after the data has been collected. The possibility of missing important data is increased because the person collecting it is unaware of analytical methods whereby the data could be meaningfully analyzed. Hence, important data may be disregarded because it seemed as if it could not be handled in any fruitful way. The possibility also increases of collecting the data in such a way as to render an otherwise critical method of analysis infeasible. The best tactic for avoiding these problems is to have the analytical alternatives in mind at the outset. This is not to say that the expert in analysis should never be consulted; but even then, a certain familiarity with the goals and computations of the alternative methods is desirable since it facilitates communication between the person compiling the data and the analytical expert.

TYPES OF DECISIONAL OPERATIONS IN THE CLINICAL SETTING

There are essentially two ways in which quantitative methods enter into clinical decision making. In the first instance, the information derived from the data analysis is taken into consideration as the decision about a course of action is being made. The results of the analysis do not in themselves indicate which decision should be made. Rather, they are used in conjunction with other considerations relevant to the problem. The information they represent facilitates the operation of arriving at a particular course of action, but the outcome from the analysis does not in itself determine the action to be taken. For example, the problem may be one of selecting a treatment of choice for a patient or a group of patients. Analysis of data pertaining to the comparative effectiveness of the alternative treatments provides an essential piece of information. However, the data analysis is integrated with a number of other considerations such as the expense of the treatment, the availability of treatment personnel, or the amenability of the treatment setting to the therapeutic procedures. The results of the analysis on comparative effectiveness participate with these other considerations to determine the final outcome, but the decision does not rest solely on the information yielded by the analysis.

This function of data analysis in the decisional operation occurs, for instance, when the clinician acts as a consultant to other clinical personnel. The consulting clinician may be asked to provide information regarding a certain aspect of a pressing problem—to ascertain the comparative effectiveness of two types of treatments. His assignment is to obtain the relevant data and carry out an analysis which answers the referred question. The decision as to which treatment to adopt resides with the referring clinician after the information obtained from the consulting clinician is taken into account. Of course, in practice, the roles of consultant and referring clinician are not so clear-cut, but the illustration serves to point out that the decision rules regarding the adoption of alternate courses of action are not built into the results of the consulting clinician's data analysis itself.

On the other hand, it is possible to directly integrate the decision rules leading to a particular course of action into the computational procedures. In this case, a certain outcome of data analysis automatically leads to one course of action and some other outcome leads to a different course of action. Included in the analysis are factors such as the relative costs and benefits of each course of action, including cost in personnel, demands on facilities, and expected benefits from more effective procedures. The decision rules are explicit in the sense that a certain outcome leads to a specific course of action. This type of decision making can be further illustrated from classification approaches. Diagnostic data including such variables as symptoms and signs, hospitalization history and demographic variables can be analyzed using an appropriate method. The results of the analysis can take the form of a number of values, each indicating the probability of the patient belonging to a corresponding diagnostic category. The patient is automatically assigned to the category with the highest probability value. The diagnostic course of action has been built into the analysis outcome. In contrast, the first approach to the use of data in decision making would take account of the probability values without considering them as the last word. Instead, these values would be integrated in some formal or informal way with other considerations prior to arriving at a final diagnosis.

The approach incorporating the decisional course of action directly into the computations is represented by the procedures in the latter part of Chapter 6, and in the section in Chapter 8 on patient classification using discriminant-function analysis. The remaining methods are geared toward the analysis of available data with an eye to obtaining information which can contribute to the decisional operation.

It should be mentioned that decision rules associated with statistical significance testing can be integrated into data analysis without directly implicating particular courses of action. In this case, the decision rules are directed toward conclusions regarding the tenability of alternate hypotheses about the state of the variables under analysis. For example, the statistical significance of the difference between treatment group means, or the significance of an obtained relationship between two variables in the form of a correlation coefficient, may be tested. The decision rules are of the form; If the probability of the differences or relations under consideration is sufficiently small, given only the influence of random effects on the dependent variables, then the hypothesis of an actual differential effect between the treatment groups, or some systematic relation between the variables, is tenable; if not, the hypothesis of no systematic treatment effect or inter-variable relation is tenable. The critical probability value is usually set prior to the analysis (for example, the conventional $p = .05$) and the probability value obtained from the analysis then compared to it. The decision rule leads to an acceptance of the first hypothesis if the obtained probability value meets the criterion, and to acceptance of the second (null) hypothesis if it does not meet the criterion value. Note that these decision rules pertain to hypotheses about the presence or absence of treatments effects or inter-variable relations. They do not spell out a course of action to be taken other than that relating to the acceptance of one or the other of these hypotheses. The decision made about the alternative hypotheses becomes a part of the constituent information entered into the decisional process pertaining to a specific course of action. In other words, the computations, in conjunction with the decision rules, have led only to a decision about one or another hypotheses regarding the variables that have been analyzed. There remains the problem of using this decision to select one of several courses of action.

Overview

The methods presented in this book are arranged to progress from patient-specific data analysis (Chapters 2 through 5), through methods involving group data on individual variables (Chapters 6 and 7), to methods for group data on multiple variables (Chapters 8 through 10). Unless the reader is familiar with vector and matrix operations, he is advised to consult the Appendices before reading Chapters 8 through 10. Readers interested only in a general description of the methods discussed in the last three chapters need not consult the Appendices if the computational formulas are disregarded.

2

Group Versus Single-Subject Approaches to Obtaining Clinically Relevant Information

Toward the end of the 1950s, clinical psychologists became increasingly interested in the possibility of adopting experimental methods in applied settings.[3,8] A traditional barrier in formulating hypotheses about a given patient's problem or some interesting clinical principle, and then testing the hypotheses, lay in the requirement of several subjects for existing research designs.[5] Thus, the publication of procedures for carrying out experiments on one subject at a time was generally welcomed among practitioners and researchers who were already convinced of the potential value of experimental methods in the clinical setting. Added to the work by clinicians in developing these procedures was the influential *Tactics of Scientific Research* by Murray Sidman[9] which not only encouraged the use of single-subject research designs in studying behavior, but took traditional group designs to task for masking important sources of behavioral variation and encouraging weak experimental control over extraneous variables. Certainly the wealth of single-subject clinical research done within the framework of applied behavioral analysis[4] is a reflection of the influence of this book.

GENERALIZABILITY OF RESULTS

Controversial issues over the use of individual versus several-subject research designs center around the applicability of results

6

from a given investigation. One of the issues involves generalization of conclusions to other subjects and is a version of the nomethetic versus idiographic dichotomy in the scientific approach to human behavior. The nomethetic approach is concerned with identifying principles relevant to large populations; the most immediate concerns of the idiographic approach are to draw inferences about the individual. (However, investigators using single-subject approaches by no means limit themselves to a restricted degree of generalization with respect to subject populations.)

The generalizability issue increases in salience when we find that the first few chapters of any group-research design text clearly indicate that statistical inference to any population of subjects requires equal probability of experimental inclusion among its constituent members. Clinicians who espouse research on groups of subjects argue that after enough information has been obtained with this approach, application to specific subjects and situations will proceed relatively easily and efficiently. The principal advantage of this route is ultimately a body of knowledge—a comprehensive "clinical technology"—impinging on each individual patient dealt with by the clinician. The principal disadvantage is the lingering question of how to treat individual patients in the interim. Medical ethics require that some treatment be administered, leaving the therapist to estimate the likelihood that a particular procedure of demonstrated efficacy for a group of subjects will better the status of his current patient.

This question can be delineated into two parts: Was the previous experimental group selected from a population to which the present patient could be considered as belonging? If it can be ascertained that the patient does belong to that population, is he representative of those members on which the treatment was effective? (The group-average value is not necessarily representative of the score for any specific member of the group contributing to that average.) The first concern relates to the issue of statistical generalization mentioned previously. The latter concern relates to the assumptions associated with analysis of variance, the most common method of statistically analyzing experimental data.

In the analysis-of-variance model, an obtained score is usually defined as a function of several additive effects. For example, the model for a simple analysis of variance is $Y = \mu + \beta_k + \epsilon_{ik}$; where μ is a constant (hypothetically the average of all observations in all referent populations); β_k is the effect of treatment k and is "constant" for all observations administered the kth treatment; and ϵ_{ik} is the error component associated with residual variation of the observation. The effect, β_k, is defined as the deviation of the mean of the kth population from μ. Suppose the kth group consists of those subjects previously administered the treatment that is currently being considered by the therapist for his patient's problem. The therapist knows only that there are grounds for believing that the kth group is not representative of a population of subjects for whom the deviation, β_k, was equal to zero. Clearly, a treatment moderately dislodging a good proportion of observations from the values they would otherwise have, or one sizeably dislodging a small number of observations from their original positions, is more than adequate to produce a nonzero treatment effect, β_k (as defined above. That effect is constant for all subjects exposed to its corresponding manipulation only in the sense that they all contribute to the same mean. Thus, the designation of a constant β_k for all subjects in group k is essentially a mathematical convenience whose purpose is to facilitate the partitioning of components of variation in the dependent variable.

In a sense, the conclusions drawn from a piece of group research leave more inferences about the treatment, that it has the capacity to shift the mean of a population to which it has been administered, than about the subjects on whom the treatment putatively had its effect. What the shift in mean implies for the individual member of the population is probably too uncertain to be of immediate practical value. In the future, the body of knowledge surrounding the treatment may be sufficient for the therapist to assess whether the "organismic" characteristics (IQ, sex, etc.) of the individual patient indicate the efficacious application of the treatment. However, for the present the clinician may opt for resolving the generalizability issue by setting his experimental hypothesis, and its corresponding test, at the patient-specific level.

INTERNAL AND EXTERNAL VALIDITY OF RESULTS

Another major aspect of any controversy surrounding the advisability of single-subject approaches is that of generalization with respect to the context in which the treatment is to be applied. Generalization from nonclinical to clinical settings can be hazardous if treatment effects depend on the coexistence of some variable intrinsic to the setting in which the experiment was carried out. This issue represents the external versus internal validity[2] of research results. Internal validity refers to whether or not a significant experimental effect can be attributed to the designated treatment as opposed to some irrelevant factor confounded with the treatment. For example, if one treatment group consisted primarily of males and another consisted primarily of females, and if the treatment of interest was unrelated to sex differences in response, the differential makeup of the groups would prevent internal validity of the conclusion that the treatment alone produced the results. The principal advantage of laboratory research is that such extraneous factors can typically be kept track of through matching treatment-irrelevant variables and random assignment of subjects to treatment levels. Hence, internal validity, in the sense of unambiguous attribution of obtained effects, is usually less at issue in the laboratory than in the clinical setting.

The problem of external validity refers to potential difficulties in generalizing conclusions to nonlaboratory situations where some of the experimentally extraneous variables, (such as location of the laboratory, room color and size, time of day, subjects' suspicions of artificiality, implicit expectations that hypotheses will be confirmed, sex of the experimenter) are no longer present. Factors disrupting external validity are those which may be constant across all treatment conditions, but whose presence is critical to the obtained treatment effects. Consider a study comparing two methods of automated systematic desensitization for phobias. One method may be very effective, but this effectiveness is lost if the apparatus delivering the treatment does not command the attention of the subject. The other method has a negligible effect regardless of the apparatus. As it happens, the apparatus delivering the treatments in the experiment has the cybernetic good fortune to be attention eliciting. The experimental results reveal the superiority of the one treatment over the other. If a different type of apparatus is used in the clinic, the treatment may be rendered ineffective and the conclusions from the experiment erroneously applied to the clinic. Similar examples are plentiful (such as the sex of the therapist in the experiment versus the sex of the therapist in the clinic).[6]

Note that the extraneous factor in this case is "a constant" as long as one restricts consideration to the laboratory itself. However, when the perspective extends beyond the experimental setting, the extraneous variable changes. The corresponding change in the configuration of experimental treatment effects constitutes the challenge to the external validity of the experiment. Clearly, the characteristics of any extraneous variable of the setting that hosts the experiment can be considered as one of several levels of that variable, the characteristics of the variable in the clinical setting being another level. Returning to the previous example, there may be a wide variety of apparatus with varying degrees of attention-eliciting properties. To the degree that the treatment effects of interest depend on the specific level of the extraneous variable present at the time of administration, the treatment *interacts* with the extraneous variable. This problem exists whenever a treatment is tested in a setting markedly different from the one in which it is to be used. The interaction is clearly an important component of the overall picture of variation in the measures of outcome. But as long as there is no more than one level of the extraneous variable in the experiment, usually the case whenever extraneous variables are "held constant", any estimation of the magnitude of the interaction is impossible. If the clinician is to apply the laboratory findings with any degree of confidence, he must be able to conclude on logical grounds that the change in level of the extraneous variable or variables will negligibly alter laboratory-established treatment effects.[7] Alternatively, he can draw this conclusion empirically by doing another experiment in the context of the specific level of the extraneous variables to be present under the conditions in which the treatment is to be used. Because clinical single-subject research is done in the treatment setting itself, its appeal is quite obvious to clinical experimenters who are concerned about external validity and willing to make at least a moderate sacrifice of internal validity.

The literature is replete with studies whose results exemplify the difficulties presented by limited external validity, as well as by generalizability. In a review by Bucher[1] an incisive analysis is made of such studies and the potential resolution of some of their problems through the adoption of single-subject approaches.

SIGNIFICANCE TESTING IN SINGLE-SUBJECT APPROACHES

One of the major obstacles encountered by users of single-subject designs has been the applicability of conventional statistics to the obtained data. The statistical issue is not one of generalizability of treatment effects to other subjects or situations, but of inferring whether an apparent treatment effect is attributable to essentially extraneous or random sources. The problem can be broken down into two components commonly referred to as "carry-over" and "auto-correlation."

Carry-over consists of the perseverating influence of the preceding imposed treatment manipulation on the dependent variable when a subsequent manipulation is being administered. Successive manipulations are confounded with what exists of the residual influence of preceding treatments. This problem is sometimes referred to as "order effects" with the perseverational influences labeled "delayed effects." It is self-evident that observations under the influence of the immediate treatment, along with the perseverating influence of preceding treatments, make for ambiguous conclusions at best.

The problem of autocorrelated observations is more subtle. Often the statistician will object to the use of conventional statistics with single subjects because the observations "are not independent." The experimenter is likely to obligingly agree with this appraisal because, after all, the observations have been obtained from the same organism. But why does the group researcher not have to be concerned when his observations are all obtained from the same experimental laboratory by the same research assistant? Are these not interdependent (autocorrelated) as well? What the statistician is really objecting to is not interdependent data, but inequality in this interdependence between different pairs of observational occasions. Unequal interdependence over time is usually attributed to fluctuations in the treatment-independent aspects of the subject's disposition (such as spontaneous changes in physical and emotional states). Influences of these dispositional factors on the dependent variable are more likely to be similar when they are temporally adjacent to each other than when they are temporally remote. The term "unequal lag correlation" is often applied to this phenomenon. It implies that observations obtained at similar times will have more in common than observations obtained at times more distant from each other.

Typically, this source of variation is randomized across treatment manipulations by randomly selecting the treatment to be administered during each observational session. However, single-subject research often requires a succession of observations under a given treatment. This requirement exists when, for example, pharmacological effects of a drug require its accumulation in the system over a period of time. It is also true of the main designs used in applied behavior analysis.[4] Due in good part to the greater similarity of temporally adjacent subject dispositions, the observations within a given treatment manipulation will generally be more similar to each other than they are to the observations of the other treatment manipulations. In this sense, the treatments are confounded with similarities and differences in certain states of the organism.

The difficulty in carrying out unbiased statistical tests under such conditions can be illustrated by referring to one of the more familiar theorems of analysis of variance. This theorem states that, in the absence of any systematic treatment effect, the variance between treatments will be a function of the effective variance within treatments. Where the within-treatment variance is σ^2 and the number of observations for each treatment is n, the expected variance in the between-treatment means will be σ^2/n. The theorem provides an essential groundwork for testing the null hypothesis that the mean variance is indeed σ^2/n, which corresponds to the hypothesis that the administered treatment effect was zero. However, if the effective between-mean variance is underestimated by the within-treatment based term, σ^2/n, prior to any effect of the treatment of interest, a bias favoring statistically significant results occurs. The coalescing influence of temporally adjacent observations prevents a true estimate of the state of affairs among the treatment means under the null hypothesis of no treatment effects. The correct expected value of mean variance is $(\sigma^2)'/n$ rather than σ^2/n. Here, $(\sigma^2)'$ represents within-group variance unaffected by the elevated coalescence associated with within-treatment proximity of observations, σ^2 is the within-group variance with the elevated coalescence intact, and $\sigma^2 < (\sigma^2)'$. Under the unbiased condition, the expected value of the F ratio would be:

$$\frac{(\sigma^2)'\chi^2/(df \text{ for numerator})}{(\sigma^2)'\chi^2/(df \text{ for denominator})} = 1$$

since the expected value of χ^2 divided by its degrees of freedom is 1. Clearly, the blending effect of within-treatment proximity of observations leads to a value greater than the usual expected value, and, correspondingly, to a positive bias:

$$\left[\frac{(\sigma^2)'(\chi^2/(df \text{ for numerator})}{\sigma^2(\chi^2(df \text{ for denominator}))}\right] > 1$$

Because of the potential advantages in using single-subject research strategies, along with the potential difficulties encountered in adopting these strategies, considerable attention has been given to various aspects of single-subject techniques. This attention has centered around the measurement of symptoms, and also on the unbiased statistical analyses of these measurements. The analyses of the measurements have been designed to overcome the problems of carry-over, to circumvent the disrupting effects of correlated observations on statistical inference, and in some instances to capitalize on interobservation correlations as an important source of clinical information. In the next chapter, some of the measurement devices developed for the individual patient are discussed.

REFERENCES

1. Bucher, B. D. Problems and prospects for psychotherapy research and design. In O. I. Lovans & B. D. Bucher (Eds.), *Perspectives in behavior modification with deviant children.* Englewood Cliffs: Prentice Hall, 1974.
2. Campbell, D. T. Factors relevant to the validity of experiments in social settings. *Psychol. Bull.,* 1957, **54,** 297–312.
3. Chassan, J. B. Statistical inference and the single case in clinical design. *Psychiat.,* 1960, **23,** 173–184.
4. Leitenberg, H. The use of single-case methodology in psychotherapy research. *J. Abnorm. Psychol.,* 1973, **82,** 87–101.
5. Lindquist, E. F. *Design and analysis of experiments in psychology and education.* Boston: Houghton Mifflin, 1953.
6. McGuigan, F. J. The experimenter: A neglected stimulus object. *Psychol. Bull.,* 1963, **60,** 421–428.
7. Neufeld, R. W. J. Generalization of results beyond the experimental setting: Statistical versus logical considerations. *Perc. and Mot. Ski.,* 1970, **31,** 443–446.
8. Shapiro, M. B. Experimental method in the psychological description of the individual psychiatric patient. *Int. J. of Soc. Psych.,* 1957, **3,** 89–102.
9. Sidman, M. *Tactics of scientific research.* New York; Basic Books, 1960.

3
Personal Questionnaire Techniques

In contrast to the familiar methods of drawing psychometric inferences by referring a subject's performance to a distribution of test scores, personalized assessment is truly an idiographic approach. The observations emanate from the patient's "response population," and reliability and validity considerations are patient-specific. The main concern of the experimenter is variation in the symptoms of the individual. Some intervention strategy is usually administered over the course of measurement. Knowledge of the patient's performance relative to an appropriate normative sample is sacrificed, since most individual questionnaires have no formalized norms—gained, however, is a larger amount of item content validity since the items themselves are often patient-generated. Patient-specific measures also afford potentially greater concurrent validity in that items are apt to be more sensitive to fluctuations in psychological states from one occasion to the next.[5] Objective estimates of reliability usually depend on measures of internal consistency in responding, and estimates of validity are somewhat more elusive.

THE SHAPIRO PERSONAL QUESTIONNAIRE

One of the earliest and still most popular of the individualized questionnaires was that of Shapiro.[10] Subsequent to its development, Shapiro demonstrated a number of ingenious methods for acquiring clinical information with this questionnaire.[11] A computerized scoring method has also been developed by Phillips.[7]

The construction of the questionnaire is quite straightforward. In the first phase, a list of the patient's symptoms are obtained and formed into a set of statements describing each symptom in the patient's own words. The relevance of the list of statements can be verified through consultation with another therapist acquainted with the patient.

In the second phase, the clinician formulates a set of statements for each symptom. The statements describe the symptom in states ranging from illness through varying degrees of improvement to recovery. At first the clinician prepares several statements for each symptom, but as greater proficiency with the technique is attained, three or four such statements should be adequate in most cases.

During the next meeting with the patient, the prepared statements are arranged along a pleasantness-disturbance continuum. This procedure is facilitated by the use of nine hedonic phrases (Table 3-1) reflecting various points on the continuum.

Each statement, typed on a card, is presented to the patient who is asked to place it beside the most closely related hedonic phrase. Three statements are then selected for each symptom: one indicating illness; one indicating improvement; and one indicating recovery. A useful rule of thumb in selecting these statements is to consider one associated with "very unpleasant" or "very great displeasure" as an illness statement; one associated with at least slight or moderate pleasantness as indicating recovery; and one between these two ranges as indicating improvement. To facilitate discriminability of statements along the hedonic continuum, it is best to have the improvement statement separated from the two adjacent statements by a distance of at least two hedonic phrases.

Table 3-1
List of Hedonic Phrases

Very great pleasure
Very pleasant
Moderately pleasant
Slightly pleasant
Indifferent
Slightly unpleasant
Moderately unpleasant
Very unpleasant
Very great displeasure

For example, the initial expression of the symptom may be, "I find difficulty in following conversations with the ward nurse." The statement representing illness may be, "Conversations with the ward nurse are utterly meaningless to me" (very unpleasant); the improvement representative may be, "Conversations with the ward nurse make hardly any sense to me" (slightly unpleasant); and the recovery representative may be, "On the whole, I can follow conversations with the ward nurse" (slightly pleasant).

The administration of the personal questionnaire involves presenting the selected statements in pairs. There are three pairs per symptom: illness–recovery, illness–improvement, and recovery–improvement. The pairs are presented in random order. On each presentation, the patient is requested to indicate which statement most closely describes his current state. The rationale behind scoring the subject's responses is depicted in Figure 3-1. The positions A, B, C, and D of the patient's symptom represent four patterns of response to the statement pairs. The A pattern indicates that the symptom is closest to the recovery statement (1). The B pattern indicates that the symptom is closest to the improvement statement (2) but on the recovery side of (2). The C pattern indicates that the symptom is closest to statement (2), but on the illness side. Finally, pattern D indicates that the symptom is closest to the illness statement (3). The patient's decision between any two statements is best viewed as a comparison between two distances along the underlying continuum. This approach is based on Coombs' unfolding model for analyzing rank-order judgments.[2]

For example, consider the pattern of responses associated with position C in Figure 3-1. As the distance between C and statement (2), d_{c2}, is less than d_{c1}, statement (2) is preferred over statement (1). The subject will select statement (2) over statement (3) for a similar reason. Finally, statement (3) being preferred to statement (1) indicates that $d_{c3} < d_{c1}$ and tells the clinician that the symptom is on the illness side of statement (2).

The scores for the upper four patterns of Table 3-2 are based on the positions of the symptom they imply according to Figure 3-1. The bottom four patterns of Table 3-2 represent inconsistent responses. For example, consider the pattern associated with an imaginary symptom position, E. If $d_{e1} < d_{e2}$, and $d_{e2} < d_{e3}$, then contrary to the response to statement pair (1)(3), d_{e3} cannot be less than d_{e1}.

If inconsistent responses occur rarely, it can be assumed that the error is essentially accidental on the part of the patient or the clinician. These inconsistencies can be scored arbitrarily according to

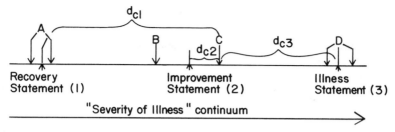

Fig. 3-1.   Positions of symptom in relation to descriptor statements.

the values in Table 3-2. However, if the proportion of inconsistent responses is relatively large (if it approaches .50) the data is probably too unreliable to score.

Such inconsistency may in itself be a symptom of psychopathology representing important clinical data. This possibility should be kept in mind not only when considering inconsistency on the Shapiro Personal Questionnaire, but also for any of the other techniques described in this chapter. Braatz's[1] measure of intransivity of items along an aversive-pleasant continuum is an excellent example of using inconsistent responding as an index of patient status. The inconsistency response index is based on patterns similar to E through H of Table 3-2. The measure was designed to indicate severity of cognitive slippage among schizophrenics.

Table 3-2
Response Patterns Corresponding to Real (A through D) and Imaginary (E through F) Symptom Positions on an Underlying Continuum.

				Severity Score
A	(1) —>— (2)	(1) —>— (3)	(2) —>— (3)	1
B	(1) —<— (2)	(1) —>— (3)	(2) —>— (3)	2
C	(1) —<— (2)	(1) —<— (3)	(2) —>— (3)	3
D	(1) —<— (2)	(1) —<— (3)	(2) —<— (3)	4
E	(1) —>— (2)	(1) —<— (3)	(2) —>— (3)	2.5
F	(1) —<— (2)	(1) —>— (3)	(2) —<— (3)	2.5
G	(1) —>— (2)	(1) —>— (3)	(2) —<— (3)	1
H	(1) —>— (2)	(1) —<— (3)	(2) —<— (3)	4

Note (1) —>— (2) indicates (1) preferred to (2), etc.

PHILLIPS' ORDINAL PERSONAL QUESTIONNAIRE

The comparisons between statements and symptom in Shapiro's technique are comparative because the patient indicates only that one distance is greater than the other in the pair. Hence, the clinician can only infer that the symptom is closer to one statement than another. The specific distance (Fig. 3-1) between the symptom and the closer statement, or the symptom and the further statement, are not available using this method. While such information is lacking, the judgments themselves are less difficult to make than the complex judgments required to retrieve the distance length. Furthermore, the likelihood of overinferring one's data, due to assuming a degree of precision unavailable to the patient, is reduced. A similar type of personal questionnaire, also based on the ordinal positions of symptom-statement distances, has been outlined by Phillips.[8]

The method of construction resembles the Shapiro Personal Questionnaire. Initially, a preliminary scaling of statements is required for each symptom considered to be clinically important. Usually four or five statements are sufficient to span the range of a symptom's severity. For example, one symptom may be "ambivalence," in that the patient finds it difficult to decide on a course of action when confronting even a minor problem. Four statements representing increasing severity of this symptom might be:

1. I seem to be able to make decisions with no problems at all.
2. I have relatively little difficulty in making decisions.
3. I can't make decisions very well.
4. I find a great deal of difficulty in making decisions even about minor matters.

The patient should confirm that the statements are to him clearly representative of increasing degrees of disturbance.

In administering the questionnaire, two marker cards are placed in front of the patient, one with the word *better* typed on it, and the other with the word *worse*. The cards are placed well apart from one another. The patient is then presented with the statements printed on cards, in random order. He is asked to indicate whether he feels better or worse than the statement on the card, and to place the card by the appropriate marker. The score is based on the degree of severity reached before the patient says he feels better than the presented statement. For example, if the patient said he felt worse than the statements (1) to (3) presented in the above example, but better than statement (4), he would be given a score of three. For convenience, "worse" responses can be indicated by a 1 on a scoring sheet, and a "better" response as zero. If the patient responds consistently, the total of these values is equal to his score. Consistent responses are indicated by a series of zero or more 1's followed by a series of zero or more 0's, as one progresses from the less to more severe statements. Inconsistent responding is indicated by any pattern departing from such a sequence.

Again, the response patterns can be illustrated by viewing the response-selection process as a paired comparison of distances. With the Shapiro Personal Questionnaire, the relevant distances were those between each statement and the symptoms. The relevant pair of distances with Phillips' ordinal method is between the symptom and one of the end poles of a worst–best continuum (Fig. 3-2), and between the statement and the end pole. For example, the symptom location in Figure 3-2 would lead to a "worse" response for each of statements (1), (2), and (3), since the distances between the "worst" end pole and these statements are greater than is the distance between the "worst" end pole and the symptom. Conversely, the distances between the "best" end pole and the statements are each less than the distance between the "best" end pole and the symptom. When the fourth statement is reached, the order of the statement and symptom distances is reversed, and a response of "better" is given.

An example of an inconsistent response pattern occurs when the patient gives a "worse" response for statements (1) and (2), a "better" response for statement (3), and a "worse" response for statement (4). This pattern indicates that the symptom is further from the "worst" end pole than statement (3) but closer than statement (4).

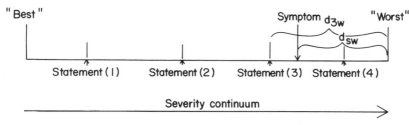

Fig. 3-2. Positions of symptom and descriptor statements in relation to end poles of the severity continuum.
Note: d_{3w} = distance between "worst" end pole and statement 3;
d_{sw} = distance between "worst" end pole and symptom.

Since statement (4) is closer to the "worst" end pole than is (3), the inconsistency is apparent.

As with the Shapiro Personal Questionnaire, a small number of such inconsistencies can be attributed to random slips. The inconsistent response patterns can be scored according to the pattern that is obtained by changing as few as possible of the patient's judgments to make the pattern consistent. For example, if the scores for statements (1) through (4) are 1,0,1,1, the pattern is changed to 1,1,1,1, yielding a score of four. When, as is often the case, either of two alterations meet the criterion of minimum change, the resulting scores can be averaged. Suppose the pattern is 1,0,1,0. This pattern can be changed to 1,1,1,0, (a score of three) or to 1,0,0,0 (a score of one) for an average of two.

Phillips[8] provided a rather elaborate method of assessing the statistical significance of the obtained number of inconsistent responses under the (null) hypothesis that the patient is responding randomly. If the questionnaire is not understood or is meaningless to the patient, each component of the better–worse dichotomy is expected to occur with equal likelihood. In other words, the probability of one or the other response is .50. If the obtained number of inconsistent responses is sufficiently unlikely (one in twenty) under this hypothetical condition, the data can be viewed as being somewhat systematic in the sense that the response distribution departs from a probability of .50. The details of the significance test are quite involved and laborious beyond practical feasibility if carried out by hand. However, computer programs are available[8] to those interested in using the test in their practice, or for research purposes. A more convenient but less rigorous method of assessing consistency is to first enumerate that proportion of all the possible response patterns for a given symptom which are inconsistent (according to the response-pattern criterion outlined above), and then to compare this value to the proportion produced by the patient. If the two proportions are similar, the patient may be respondingly randomly.

In comparing his method of ordinal scaling to that of Shapiro's, Phillips noted that the judgmental points of reference for his questionnaire are the statements themselves, whereas with Shapiro's method, they are essentially the midpoints between the statements. Phillips showed that the latter points of reference can lead to reduced sensitivity to symptom change when the symptom is initially located at an extreme of the severity continuum. His method overcomes this difficulty.

PHILLIPS' INTERVAL PERSONAL QUESTIONNAIRE

As mentioned, the methods of comparative judgments outlined previously provide estimates of the relative positions of statements and the symptom on the underlying continuum. They do not allow more discrete estimates of locations on the continuum. For instance, in the example depicted in Figure 3-2 we can ascertain that the symptom lies somewhere between statement (3) and statement (4). However, any position between statements (3) and (4) would give us the same information. Yet, it might be informative to know that the symptom lies about $1/3$ of the way up the continuum between the two statements in contrast to $7/8$ of the way up. Better still would be the availability of numerical values corresponding to the symptom's and the statements' relative positions on the continuum. Estimates of these values are available with interval methods of scaling.[9]

Once again, a list of statements associated with a given symptom is drawn up with the patient. To facilitate this procedure, a description of the symptom should be elicited from the patient and statements implying varying degress of intensity constructed. The statements should be comprehensible to the patient and should have the varying degrees of clearly perceptible intensity intended. For example, a patient with kidney failure was referred to a clinician because of difficulty in sleeping. Due to the nature of her illness, her physician was reluctant to increase her nightly dosage of sedation. Two additional problems, seemingly correlated with the sleep problem, were present. One was increasingly strained marital relations and the second was a fear of losing a transplanted kidney through lack of proper rest.

The treatment of choice was to give practice in Jacobsonian relaxation exercises combined with instructions to carry them out prior to retirement each evening. In a case such as this one the interval scaling method could be used to monitor the patient's difficulty in sleeping over the course of treatment as well as to test the clinical hypothesis that severities of the other two problems were related to that of the sleeping problem. An approximate test of this hypothesis could be obtained through calculating correlations among the interval symptom values across occasions of testing.

In the present case, the statements for the sleep symptom itself are:

1. I have no difficulty in sleeping at night.
2. I find it slightly difficult to sleep at night.

3. I find that it is hard to drop off to sleep at night.
4. I find that sleeping at night comes with considerable difficulty.
5. I find it extremely difficult to sleep at night.
6. I find it impossible to sleep at night.

Administration of this questionnaire can make use of preliminary scaling of the statements or it can proceed without preliminary scaling. If the questionnaire is to be administered a relatively large number of times $(3(p - 1)$, where p is the number of statements for the given symptom), preliminary scaling will probably not change the final estimates of the statement scale values enough to warrant the additional computational effort. However, if the questionnaire is to be administered a relatively small number of times, or if the clinician is unsure as to how many administrations will be feasible, preliminary scaling can add substantially to the validity of the statement scale values.

In order to obtain the preliminary estimates, the two extreme statements (for example, (1) and (6) of the above set) are placed apart from each other in front of the patient. An arbitrary quantity (100) is assigned to the interval between them. Then all pairs of statements, except those involving the uppermost extreme, (6), are presented. The patient is asked to indicate which of the pair denotes more severity, and by how much, on the hypothetical interval of 100. The uppermost statement is sacrificed in the paired comparison ratings because it is meaningless to include it with the lowermost statement when the interval has already been assigned a score of 100. A $(p - 1)$ $\times (p - 1)$ matrix is constructed, as is illustrated in Table 3-3, where each number indicates the degree of judged separation between the statement directly above and directly to the left. The numbers are given a negative sign if the statement in the *column* of the value indicates less severity and a positive sign if the statement in the *row* of the value indicates less severity. This matrix is symetric (see Appendix B) in that the values in row i and column j are identical to those in row j and column i (where $i, j = 1, 2, \ldots, (p - 1)$, except for sign.

The establishing of interval scale values in this type of personal questionnaire capitalizes on an important property of each column and row of values. The judgments in each column are constant with respect to the specific statement they "revolve around," this statement being at the top of the column. In addition, each row of judgments is constant with regard to the statement which its values

Table 3-3
Preliminary Scaling of Statements.

	No	Slight	Hard	Consid-erable	Extreme	
	(1)	(2)	(3)	(4)	(5)	
(1) No difficulty		8	47	65	83	
(2) Slight difficulty	−8		33	54	75	
(3) Hard to drop off	−47	−33		17	37	
(4) Considerable difficulty	−65	−54	−17		23	
(5) Extreme difficulty	−83	−75	−37	−23		Total
Total	−203	−154	26	113	218	0
Preliminary Estimate	−40.6	−30.8	5.2	22.6	43.6	0
Combined-Estimate Scaling of Statements						
Total from above	−203	−154	26	113	218	
Row sum from Table 3-4 ($X(-1)$)	−637	−477	31	318	620	Mean
Grand total	−840	−631	57	431	838	−29
Standardized Grand Total	−811	−602	86	460	867	
Final Estimate	−40.55	−30.1	4.3	23	43.35	

revolve around, that statement being to the left. The set of statements serving as judgmental referents is constant in each row and each column, provided the statement at the top or at the left is itself considered a part of this set. So considered, the diagonals of the matrix are zero since the distance of a statement from itself is zero. These properties will become clearer with the algebraic descriptions of the judgments provided here.

Hence, as one moves from row to row, there is a shift in the specific statement participating in all the judgments located in the row but not in the referent statements to which the left-hand statement has been compared. This shift also occurs with respect to the statements heading each column, as one moves from column to column. Thus, the changes among row and column averages reflect the differences in scale values between the statements heading the rows or the columns. For example, the expected value of the column total for statement (1) will be:

$$(3.1) \qquad \sum_{j=1}^{p-1} x_{1j} = \sum_{j=1}^{p-1} (s_1 - s_j) = (p - 1)s_1 - \sum_{j=1}^{p-1} s_j$$

Clinical Quantitative Methods

Table 3-4
Symptom Judgments over 5 Statements and 15 Occasions.

Statement Occasions	1	2	3	4	5	6	7
(1) No difficulty	80	90	60	67	50	53	73
(2) Slight difficulty	63	75	50	55	37	45	64
(3) Hard to drop off	40	40	12	23	5	10	32
(4) Considerable difficulty	17	25	−6	0	−13	−10	12
(5) Extreme difficulty	−5	8	−28	−20	−37	−30	−8
Total	195	238	88	125	42	68	173
Estimate	39	47.6	17.6	25	8.4	13.6	34.6

Total: 145. Means of Sums: 29.

where x_{1j} is the judgment corresponding to $(s_1 - s_j)$;
s_1 is the scale value for statement 1 on the underlying continuum;
and s_j is the scale value for statement j on the underlying continuum.

The expected value of the mean will be:

$$s_1 - (1/p - 1) \left(\sum_{j=1}^{p-1} s_j \right)$$

with the latter term denoting the average scale value for all $p - 1$ statements. Since this latter term will be a constant (c) for all columns, the difference between the mean of column 1 and that of any other column j will provide a ready estimate of the difference in scale values between the statements 1 and j. Specifically, $(s_1 - c) - (s_j - c) = s_1 - s_j$.

Because the selected metric (a distance of 100 between the extreme statements) is initially arbitrary, only the relative positions of the statements and the relative intervals between them are of any real interest. That is, while a value of 30 for s_1 is meaningless, a value of 30 for the distance between s_1 and a given s_j can be very meaningful if the comparative value between s_1 and a different s_j is 60. Notice that the value denoted c is of no real consequence since it does not enter into the comparative numerical indices.

A similar rationale accompanies the derivation of statement values on the basis of responses from several occasions; and of the scale values for the designated symptom corresponding to each

Table 3-4   (Continued).

8	9	10	11	12	13	14	15	Sum	Standard-ized Row Sum	Final Estimate
40	33	37	32	6	8	8	0	637	608	−40.5
30	23	28	22	−3	0	0	−12	477	448	−29.9
0	−9	−12	−13	−41	−36	−35	−47	−31	−60	4.0
−20	−32	−25	−33	−58	−52	−55	−68	−318	−347	23.1
−40	−53	−46.	−53	−79	−73	−73	−83	−620	−649	43.3
10	−38	−18	−45	−175	−153	−155	−210			
2	−7.6	−3.6	−9	−35	−30.6	−31	−42			

occasion of questionnaire presentation. In administering the questionnaire on a given occasion, the patient is presented with the extreme statements, (1) and (p) (where in our current example, $p = 6$), with the indication of 100 points between the two. The patient is then presented with each of the $p − 1$ test statements in random order, and asked to indicate if the present severity of his symptom is better or worse than that indicated by the test statement. He is also asked to supply a numerical value indicating by how many points on the scale of 100 the one is better or worse than the other. The value is given a negative sign whenever the statement is worse than the symptom. These values are entered into the column for that occasion (Table 3-4). The estimate of the current symptom value is taken as the mean of the column of judgment numbers. The expected value of this mean is:

$$(3.2) \qquad \frac{1}{p-1}\sum_{j=1}^{p-1} X_{jk} = s_k - \frac{1}{p-1}\sum_{j=1}^{p-1} s_j$$

where x_{jk} is the judgment corresponding to $(s_k − s_j)$;
s_k is the position of the symptom on occasion k;
and s_j is the position of statement j.

A final estimate of each statement value is given by $(−1) \times$ (the mean of the corresponding row values of Table 3-4). These estimates can be combined with the preliminary estimates by adding the preliminary and the final totals (the latter with sign reversed) and dividing the sum by the number of occasions (n) plus the number of relevant statements ($p − 1$) (as done in the lower portion of Table 3-3).

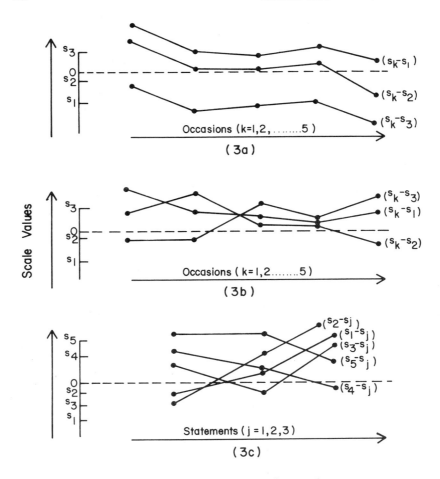

Fig. 3-3.   Scale values across occasions and statements.

For convenience of interpretation, the final estimates in Table 3-4 can each be referred to an arbitrary mean of zero (standardized mean) by subtracting the mean of the row sums for the statements from each individual sum prior to dividing by the number of occasions. In the case of the combined estimate in Table 3-3, the mean of the summed totals can be subtracted from the respective sums before dividing by $n + p - 1$.

Consistent responding is defined as any pattern that indicates the same relative positions of statements regardless of testing occasion, and the same relative positions of the symptom for the several occasions regardless of the statement of reference. Figure 3-(3a) presents a perfectly consistent response pattern. Figure 3-(3b) depicts unreliability with respect to the occasion values over the statements; and Figure 3-(3c) depicts unreliability of the statement values across the several occasions. A statistical test, Tukey's test for nonadditivity[12] (described in most basic texts on research design) can be carried out to determine the degree of unreliability. It tests for whether the actual judgments depart significantly from what would be expected on the basis of the statement and occasion values estimated according to the procedures of Table 3-4.

As a visual aid in interpreting the progress of a consistently responding patient, the estimated scale value of the symptom can be plotted. Occasions lie along the abscissa and the underlying severity continuum lies along the ordinate. The estimated scale values for the statements can be indicated on the ordinate to aid interpretation.

RATIO SCALING OF SYMPTOMS

Ratio scaling also permits estimation of the location of symptoms and statements on the underlying continuum of severity. The subject is asked to judge by what ratio the higher item, either symptom or statement, is greater than the lower item. The procedures outlined for the preceding interval method can be easily extended to the ratio method when the similarity of rationale for computed scale values is understood. Each ratio judgment is translated into the form, "The symptom represents twice ($1/3$, 4 times, etc.) the severity of the statement." Because the values are most easily treated as products, the ratio judgments can conveniently be converted to log values (to the base 10). The antilog of the average log judgment in each column of the $p \times p$ matrix, (analogous to the $p - 1 \times p - 1$ matrix of Table 3-3) serves as the estimated scale value for the corresponding column statement. The antilog of the average log judgment in each column of the $p \times n$ matrix (analogous to the $p - 1 \times n$ matrix of Table 3-4) provides an estimate of the symptom severity for that occasion. The rationale for these estimates can be illustrated by considering the antilog of the average log judgment for occasion k in relation to the p statements:

(3.3) $\text{Antilog}\left(\frac{1}{p}\sum_{j=1}^{p}X_{kj}\right) = \left\{s_k{}^p\left[\left(\frac{1}{s_1}\right)\left(\frac{1}{s_2}\right)\left(\frac{1}{s_3}\right)\cdots\left(\frac{1}{s_p}\right)\right]\right\}^{1/p} = s_k(c)$

where x_{kj} is the log of the judgment corresponding to s_{k/s_j},

and c is a scalar, and is constantly $\left(\prod_{j=1}^{p}\frac{1}{s_j}\right)^{1/p}$

An assessment of the internal consistency of responding can be obtained on the basis of occasion values from several different judgments. For example, an estimate of the ratio of symptom severity for occasion k to occasion $k + 1$ can be obtained. The antilog of the average log judgment for occasion k is divided by the antilog of the average log judgment for occasion $k + 1$. The k to $k + 1$ ratio of severity can also be estimated by dividing the value in row j of column k by the value in row j of column $k + 1$. Thus, $p + 1$ of such ratio estimates can be obtained for each pair of occasions. As the similarity among these ratios increases, so does internal consistency.

Qualifying Note on Illustrative Formulas

The illustrative formulas (3.1), (3.2), and (3.3) should be treated with some caution. They have been simplified in order to expedite the discussion of rationale behind the respective computations of scale values. The right-hand terms of the equations represent what would be obtained with errorless judgments. In this sense, they are the *expected* values of the computations, but not necessarily the *obtained* values of the computations. There is usually a degree of error in the subjective reports used for any scaling solution, and this error component offsets the obtained values from the quantities indicated by the right-hand terms of the equations used here. The effects of such error are evident when comparing the obtained judgments (for example those in the $(p - 1) \times (p - 1)$ matrix of Table 3-3 or those in the $(p - 1) \times n$ matrix of Table 3-4) with the values reproduced using the estimated scale values for statements and/or occasions. Only under errorless conditions will the two sets of values agree perfectly.

Clearly, if errors in judgment were of no consequence, the mean values of the statement–symptom judgments could be dispensed with. The relative positions of the statements could be inferred from the set of judgments obtained on any one of the n occasions; and the relative positions of the symptom for the various occasions could be inferred from the n judgments associated with any one of the set of statements.

The advantage in using mean values lies in the tendency for the effects of judgment error on scale-value estimates to diminish with a pooling of observations. The errors are assumed to be normally and independently distributed around the "true" symptom and statement scale values. This assumption is necessarily a simplifying one in that it facilitates the computations by reducing the complexity of the underlying rationale. There is reason to believe, from both clinical lore and research evidence, that patients may systematically overrate or underrate their clinical status or the implications of the statements, depending on their current severity of illness. However, in most cases the disruptive effects of such sources will probably not be large enough to dislodge the distribution of judgmental error from at least a close approximation of the assumed distribution, or to justify abandoning the development of computational procedures and the advantages accrued by allowing the simplifying assumptions to stand.

SOME FINAL CONSIDERATIONS

It should be apparent that the more refined types of estimates available from interval and ratio scaling have the distinct disadvantage of requiring somewhat precise judgments on the part of the patient. Such judgments may well be out of reach for many psychotic patients since a marked feature of schizophrenia is cognitive deficit[6] and at least a common secondary feature of depression is retardation in information processing.[4] Unless the clinician is especially interested in inconsistant responding as a measure of thought disorder, he is not advised to use the more demanding questionnaires for such patients. Instead, the comparative judgments associated with the ordinal methods are indicated. At this time, there is little to replace clinical expertise in tailoring the difficulty of response to the patient's extant psychological status, while capturing the maximum information possible about the fluctuation in symptom severity. There is little point in attempting to gain interval or ratio data when the patient is conveying ordinal information at best. One method of deciding on the level of scaling to carry out is to present the patient with several judgments from each type of questionnaire, and to settle on a type he is clearly comfortable with answering.

While the patient's psychological status may limit the level of questionnaire available to the clinician, other sources of inconsistent responding can be attributed to incorrect initial construction of the questionnaire. The two main sources are likely to be an erroneous original ordering of the statements along the underlying continuum; or, if ordered correctly, an insufficient amount of distance between the statements on the continuum preventing clear discriminability between adjacent pairs. These sources of error can be corrected by reviewing the statements with the patient.

In many instances, the clinician may not be interested in anything beyond ordinal data. He may simply wish to know when the symptom is consistently reported as remitted. In this case, he may adopt a criterion that the symptom be reported as less severe than a designated recovery statement on four consecutive occasions. On the other hand, if he is researching a new treatment technique, he may want the most sensitive instrument available for detecting slight changes in symptom severity. The selection of a personal questionnaire is like the selection of any other assessment tool. It requires the integration of a thorough knowledge of the query at hand and familiarity with methodological options available to gain the required information.

One of the deterrents from adopting the use of personal questionnaires on a routine basis may be a suspicion that an inordinate amount of time and/or expense is involved. In fact, required materials include only some index cards. The clerical aspects of construction can be carried out quickly by a secretary. The time for administering the questionnaire on each occasion is very short and well repaid by the precise information available almost immediately, with the help of an inexpensive desk calculator. Initial construction also takes little time and affords a means of establishing a certain amount of rapport with the patient. Many practitioners consider the patient's involvement in constructing his own assessment device to be clinically desirable.

The problem of validity is difficult to resolve since the estimates available to the clinician are based on the patient's own reports. Because the judgments are taken more or less at face value, there is considerable potential for the patient to fake "good" or "bad" depending, for example, on whether or not he wants to remain in the treatment institution. However, problems of bias including "acquiescence" and "social desirability" are large contributors to response variance on some of the most widely used assessment devices such as the MMPI.[3] Typically, clinicians must obtain a picture of their patient's disposition using many sources of information additional to the patient's own verbal report. The personal questionnaire makes the important contribution of allowing a much more precise and objective assessment of how the patient sees his own symptoms. The relative weight placed on subjective reports may vary with the theoretical orientation of the clinician. Regardless of theoretical orientation, the weight is necessarily reduced as precision declines in estimating what the patient is attempting to communicate to the therapist.

A partial solution to problems encountered with patients who find it difficult to spontaneously express themselves on clinical questionnaires is to have the administrations carried out by an institutional staff member, such as a nurse or occupational therapist, with whom the patient can be candid.

Another potential difficulty with personal questionnaire techniques is that of carry-over of responding. For example, the patient may remember his previous responses and try to reproduce these. (However, this problem is in no way unique to personal questionnaires.) If the patient is fabricating prior response patterns, a certain masking of the concurrent state of the symptom can be expected. Another consequence can be difficulty in statistical evaluation of the configuration of judgments. Occasions in close proximity are likely to resemble each other to a greater extent than occasions more remote from each other. If different therapies are each administered during blocks of successive occasions, a positive bias (inflated significance) of the statistical test for treatment effects can be expected. This bias is associated with the autocorrelation effect described in Chapter 2. It disrupts the unambiguous interpretation of statistical significance tests when the occasion scale values form the dependant variable. For the type of data presented in Table 3-4, the clinician may wish to test the significance of severity change over the n occasions. He may decide to submit the data to a $(p - 1) \times n$ analysis of variance. Once again, the test will be positively biased by unequal similarities in the patterns of the $p - 1$ judgments among the various pairs of occasions. Thus, the personal questionnaire can lead to difficulties in statistical inference.

But these difficulties accompany any long-term monitoring of patient status using formalized assessment techniques. Attempts at handling problems of statistical interpretation are outlined in Chapter 4. It cannot be overemphasized that as in other testing situations, the clinician must make every effort to create an atmosphere conducive to accurate responding on the part of the patient. No amount of statistical ingenuity can equal the improvement in data veracity from such efforts.

Perhaps the main advantages of personal questionnaires are their content validity. They are focused on the individual patient's symptoms. A by-product of the increased content validity should be more immediate treatment implications from the information obtained, as well as heightened sensitivity to shifts in the symptoms addressed. The clinician can identify, with little effort, areas of daily practice in which these techniques are apt to prove useful. In addition, he may find that they are ideal for his research purposes. It is well known that clinicians are often limited with respect to availability of subjects. Moreover, they typically wish to specify comprehensively the characteristics of patients for whom the research manipulations have had their most pronounced effect. Scholarly journal space is increasingly devoted to the publication of such case studies.

REFERENCES

1. Braatz, G. A. Preference intransivity as an indicator of cognitive slippage in schizophrenia. *J. Abnorm. Psychol.*, 1970, **75**, 1–6.
2. Coombs, C. H. The theory and methods of social measurement. In L. Festinger & D. Katz (Eds.), *Research methods in behavioral sciences*. New York: Dryden Press, 1953.
3. Messick, S., & Jackson, D. N. Judgmental dimensions of psychopathology. *J. Consult. Clin. Psychol.*, 1972, **38**, 418–427.
4. Miller, W. T. Psychological deficit in depression. *Psychol. Bull.*, 1975, **82**, 238–260.
5. Neufeld, R. W. J., Rogers, T. B., & Costello, C. G. Comparison of measures of depression by the experimental investigation of single cases. *Psychol. Rep.*, 1972, **31**, 771–775.
6. Payne, R. W. Cognitive abnormalities. In H. J. Eysenck (Ed.), Handbook of abnormal psychology (2nd ed.). San Diego: Knapp, 1973.
7. Phillips, J. P. N. A scheme for computer scoring a Shapiro personal questionnaire. *Br. J. Soc. Clin. Psychol.*, 1968, **7**, 309–310.
8. Phillips, J. P. N. A further type of personal questionnaire. *Br. J. Soc. Clin. Psychol.*, 1970, **9**, 338–346.
9. Phillips, J. P. N. A new type of personal questionnaire. *Br. J. Soc. Clin. Psychol.*, 1970, **9**, 241–256.
10. Shapiro, M. B. A method of measuring psychological changes specific to the individual psychiatric patient. *Br. J. Med. Psychol.*, 1961, **34**, 151–155.
11. Shapiro, M. B. The measurement of clinically relevant variables. *J. Psychosom. Res.*, 1964, **8**, 245–254.
12. Tukey, J. W. One degree of freedom for nonadditivity. *Biom.*, 1949, **5**, 232–242.

4
Statistical Inference in the Single Case

The topic of statistical inference in the single case usually refers to the testing of data obtained from an experiment performed on a single individual for statistical significance. As mentioned in Chapter 2, the use of an individual subject can usually jeopardize the validity of the obtained significance level of the test. Thus, researchers using the single-case strategy have expended considerable effort in dealing with these problems.

Single-subject statistical inference can also refer to data obtained within the context of psychometric measurement. Clinicians commonly encounter a divergence in the scores for a given individual between two tests putatively measuring the same traits or abilities or between two tests tapping different traits or abilities. If the tests are addressed to different traits or abilities, the clinician may wish to know if the divergence obtained in a particular instance can reasonably be attributed to genuine differences in the measured dimensions or instead, to test unreliability or error of measurement. If it can be concluded that the divergence represents some systematic difference in the measured dimensions, the clinician may wish to know how often a difference of the obtained size occurs in the normal population. These issues can be approached by using appropriate tests for the statistical significance of test divergence described in the latter part of the chapter.

SIGNIFICANCE TESTING OF TREATMENT MANIPULATIONS

An issue of much heated debate among clinical researchers during the last decade has been whether or not to test single-case data for the statistical significance of apparent treatment effects. Often, the debate has contributed as much confusion as elucidation of the central issues. It is common for researchers, weary of jaded arguments from exponents of both views, to consider the option of ignoring the issue and getting on with the business of acquiring data (using nonstatistical inference strategies) a more fruitful alternative than engaging in the seemingly unresolvable debate. Unfortunately, electing this option raises other questions centering around such problems as what constitutes interresearcher agreement about the presence or absence of treatment effects when the data do not clearly meet nonstatistical criteria such as those commonly employed in applied behavioral analysis. Moreover, there is no ready method of assessing the extent to which the autocorrelation effect (referred to in Chapter 2) on some graph of the data may be deluding a researcher's nonstatistical judgment into an impression of enhanced potency of a given treatment manipulation.*

Statistical analysis of single-case data can be ignored but this practice may not always be safe. At the other end of the scale, some clinicians may elect to routinely evaluate their data statistically. Still others may wish to use statistical analyses on some occasions but not on others. An awareness of the available methods and the problems to which they are addressed should facilitate the decisions of those falling into the latter category.

The present discussion will usually refer to the single case as the *single patient* or *client*. However, the present considerations can be extrapolated to the more general case where data consists of a number of observations taken on any single entity over time. This entity may be something as global as an entire treatment unit with the observations possibly being its intake-to-discharge ratio obtained at monthly intervals. Observational entities as large as a treatment setting may become the focus of data acquisition at an increasing rate, considering the mounting constraints placed upon clinicians to engage in treatment-program evaluation.[5]

---

* For a more detailed description of this controversy, the reader is referred to the series of articles in the *Journal of Applied Behavior Analysis*, 1974, Volume 7, pages 627–653.

RANDOM ASSIGNMENT OF TREATMENTS OVER TIME

An important distinction, often not made in single-case research, is the separation between procedures which allow the random assignment of a treatment during a given observational session versus those which disallow such random assignment. For example, the clinician may be interested in the comparative effectiveness of two approaches to his patient. One may be a "rational treatment" where learning principles relevant to symptom acquisition are simply explained and the other may be a form of nondirective therapy.[19] The measure of effectiveness may be a scale value for severity of an important symptom based on one of the personal questionnaires discussed in Chapter 3. If the clinician can select the treatment of choice for a forthcoming session using a random-number table or some similar device, the statistical interpretation of comparative effectiveness can be greatly simplified. Under these conditions, the clinician still faces the problem of confounding due to carry-over, but the problems of unequal correlations among observations are greatly reduced.

Chassan[3] was one of the first clinical researchers to suggest the use of a conventional statistical test to compare two treatments (drugs) randomly administered over time. Although the treatments are randomly administered, observations closer together in time are still more likely to resemble each other than they are to resemble temporally remote observations (the autocorrelation effect). However, since treatment administration bears a random relationship to points in time during the span of the research, the homogenizing of temporally proximal observations by treatment-irrelevant factors is as likely to affect data points between treatments as it is data points within treatments. Chassan's[3] procedure began by removing the linear trend in the data associated with the passage of time. The coefficient of regression of the dependent variable onto the time of observation was computed along with the intercept. (The particular treatment to which the observations belonged was temporarily ignored.) The values predicted from the regression equation using the obtained regression coefficient and intercept were then subtracted from the observed values leaving deviations from the predicted values. The deviation scores were then divided according to the corresponding treatment and a t test was applied to the difference between the two deviation-score means.

As stated above, this method does not allow for the problem of carry-over effects between the two treatments. For example, treatment *A* may have a significantly greater therapeutic effect than treatment *B* according to the *t* test on means. However, this effect has occurred in the context of the additional administration of treatment *B* during other randomly selected occasions, and not in isolation of any other treatment. It is possible that the two treatments administered independently of one another may not be differentially effective. The clinician is usually interested in using the results of research on treatment outcome so as to select one or the other treatment for an immediate problem. If the effects of treatment *A* depend on the coexistent administration of treatment *B* during other occasions, the clinician may erroneously adopt it as the procedure of choice under the false assumption that its superior effects are maintained under conditions when it is the sole treatment.

To illustrate, suppose the problem facing the patient is an inability to sleep because of anxiety associated with some aspect of his occupation. Treatment *A* may consist of systematic desensitization and treatment *B*, a "control treatment," may consist simply of Jacobsonian-type relaxation exercises. It is possible that treatment *A* may be effective only when the patient has been initiated with a session of treatment *B*, and that such sessions have been uniquely responsible for the significant difference according to the *t* test on the two means. It is apparent that some test for this type of treatment interdependence is desirable.

The following procedure is suggested for testing not only the comparative effects of two treatment alternatives in the single case, but also for the enhancing or diminishing effect of the one treatment on the effect of the other. Initially, the order of treatment administration is randomly determined by producing a pattern such as that displayed in Table 4-1. The data is then partitioned into a 2 × 2 table as illustrated in Table 4-2. The rows of the table represent the treatment administered on the occasion during which the observation was obtained, and the columns represent the treatment administered on the preceding occasion. This method assumes that any interdependence among treatment occasions is most pronounced if they are

Table 4-1.
Randomized Sequence of Two Treatments, A and B.

Occasion	1	2	3	4	5	6	7	8	9	10	11	12	13	14	15	16	17
Treatment	A	B	B	A	A	B	A	A	B	B	A	A	B	A	A	B	A

Occasion	18	19	20	21	22	23	24	25	26	27	28	29	30	31	32	33	34	35
Treatment	A	B	B	A	B	A	B	B	A	A	A	B	A	B	B	A	B	B

Table 4-2.
Cell Sizes in a 2 × 2 Table Based on the
Pattern of Table 4-1.

		Preceding Treatment		
		A'	B'	
Occasion	A	7	10	$\Sigma = 17$
Treatment	B	11	6	$\Sigma = 17$
		$\Sigma = 18$	$\Sigma = 16$	34

immediately adjacent, as opposed to being separated by still other treatment occasions. The observation from the first treatment session (for example, the first occasion of Treatment A in Table 4-1) is omitted from the analysis. It is unlikely that the 4 cells of the 2 × 2 table will have an equal number of values since the specific treatment following a given other treatment is randomly determined.

In order to handle the problem of unequal observations, it is necessary to use a nonorthogonal analysis of variance (ANOVA) procedure.[1,15] This procedure requires both conventional computations as well as a regression approach to ANOVA. The conventional analyses are generally familiar and can be found in most standard statistical texts.[11] The regression approach is probably less familiar to most clinicians. Details of computations are beyond the scope of this discussion* and can be found elsewhere.[1,16,17] Available computer programs for this analysis include Biomedical Package IOV[6], MULTIVARIANCE[7], and MANOVA.[4] The dual approach to the analysis is required because unequal cell numbers can confound the test for a columns main effect with the rows main effect and/or the row-columns interaction. In addition, the test on the rows main effect can be confounded with the columns main effect and/or the interaction.

---

* Basically, a typical regression approach computes a squared multiple correlation coefficient (outlined in Chapter 8) treating the dependent variable as the predicted variable and the main and interaction components of the independent variables as the predictors. The independent contribution of each predictor can be determined by comparing the squared multiple correlation with the predictor excluded, to that obtained with the predictor included. The sum of squares can then be calculated for each predictor by multiplying the difference in the squared multiple correlations by the value for the total sum of squares in the experiment. The error term is obtained by multiplying the total sum of squares by the quantity of one minus the squared multiple correlation with all predictors included.

The cell sizes in Table 4-2 can be used to illustrate this problem. The mean of the first row, corresponding to treatment A, is affected by more observations under column B' than column A'. The opposite is true for the second row corresponding to treatment B. Hence, a comparison of the row means will include differences in the A' versus B' effects along with any effects associated with A versus B. The regression approach has the advantage of removing the confound by testing the main effect of one factor while eliminting the main effect of the opposite factor. The conventional approach does not remove the confound since it ignores the main effect of one factor while testing the main effect of the other.

The first step in the analysis is to test the row-columns interaction. If significant, tests of the main effects are not appropriate. The significant interaction indicates that the effects of a treatment on a given occasion are influenced by the specific treatment administered during the preceding occasion. The cell means can then be examined so as to determine which preceding treatment has tended to enhance or diminish the effects of which current treatment. Using our previous illustration, the means of Table 4-3 indicate that both desensitization (treatment A) as well as Jacobsonian relaxation (treatment B) are enhanced when preceded by treatment B. Moreover, treatments A and B are not significantly discriminable from each other when they are preceded by treatment B. The configuration of results indicates that the treatment of choice for the present problem is treatment B. If administered in isolation of treatment A, it will of course follow the desired pattern of always being preceded by itself.

If the interaction is not significant, tests for the rows effect eliminating the columns effect and tests for the columns effect eliminating the rows effect are carried out using the regression approach to nonorthogonal ANOVA. If both tests are significant, the appropriate conclusion is that there is a differential effect of the treatments administered on a given occasion and there is also a differential effect of the treatments administered on the preceding occasion. If only one of the tests is significant, the corresponding part of this conclusion is retained.

If neither test is significant, the conventional ANOVA is carried out on the main effects of rows and on the main effects of columns. If both tests are significant, the conclusion allows for a rows effect or a columns effect, but not both. Typically, the choice is indeterminate; however, in the present type of design, where one of the factors is the immediate treatment and the other factor is the preceding treatment, logical considerations would ordinarily favor attributing the signifi-

Table 4-3.
Significant Rows-Columns Interaction:
Hypothetical Means.

| | | Preceding Treatment | |
		A'	B'
Occasion	A	4	6
Treatment	B	3	6

cant result to the immediate-treatment factor. If only one of the tests is significant, it may be concluded that there has been a differential treatment effect somewhere, but identification of whether it is due to the immediate-occasion or the preceding-occasion treatments, or some combination of the two, will probably require further experimentation where cell sizes are not severely imbalanced. If neither test is significant, it is concluded that no effect has occurred.*

Unlike Chassan's *t*-test procedure, the present method has thus far not partialled out the trend in the data associated with the passage of time. In the present design, this can be easily done by simply introducing time of the observation as a covariate and applying analysis of covariance. If the treatment occasions are equally spaced, the ordinal number of the occasion can be used. The design is then simply a case in point of a nonorthogonal completely randomized two-by-two factorial analysis of covariance. Most investigators have had contact with the orthogonal version of this design.[12,21] The regression approach to nonorthogonal ANOVA discussed above easily accommodates a covariate such as the passage of time.

NONRANDOM ASSIGNMENT OF TREATMENTS OVER TIME

In a great deal of single-case research, treatments are arbitrarily administered on given occasions. The investigator may have decided on a particular schedule a priori—decisions may be made about treatment administration as the data is coming in during the study as, for example, if a stable baseline is desired prior to some interven-

---

* Occasionally, a situation may arise where the test on rows eliminating columns (using the regression approach) is significant, but the test on rows ignoring columns (using the conventional approach) is nonsignificant. O'Brien[15] has provided a procedure for handling such a special case should it arise.

tion—or the pattern of treatments may be determined by the availability of observational occasions with the optimal schedule being mathematically determined.[8] Each of these procedures represents a case in point of nonrandom treatment assignment over time.

Among the more popular research designs falling into the category of nonrandom assignment are reversal designs, withdrawal designs, multiple baseline designs[13] and time-lagged control designs.[10] In each case, several observations are taken successively during each treatment phase to be compared to other treatment phases. The autocorrelation effect may inflate the significance of conventional statistical tests in such cases. The logic behind the expectation of potentially inflated significance is discussed in Chapter 2.

Among the methods proposed for handling the autocorrelation effect, those developed by John Gottman and his colleagues[9] appear to be the most appropriate in the present context. Their procedures establish a best estimate of the interdependence among the observations and take account of this estimate in establishing their statistical tests. The tests consist of t values which assess the significance of differences in the elevation of the dependent variable as well as the significance of differences in the linear trend of the data between different phases of treatment. (Figs. 4-1 and 4-2).

It is assumed that several observations are available for each phase. The more observations that are available, the greater are the number of degrees of freedom for the t tests; in that sense, the greater the sensitivity or power of the statistical assessment for determining

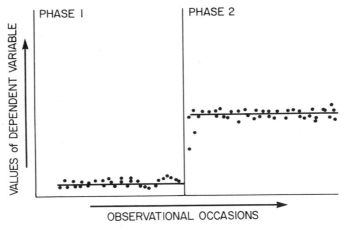

Fig. 4-1.   Significant difference in level over treatment phases.

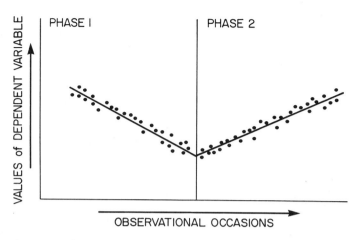

Fig. 4-2. Significant difference in slope over treatment phases.

actual treatment differences. It is assumed that the trend of the change in the data within a given treatment phase is linear—that is, the systematic changes in the data within a given period can be adequately described by a straight line. The actual analysis is computationally complex and requires a computer program provided by Gottman and his colleagues.[9] However, the goals of the analysis are quite straightforward. Through what is essentially a trial-and-error method, a summary statistic for the degree of interdependence among the observations in the study is estimated. The t values of interest are those corresponding to this best estimate. Each is tested with degrees of freedom equalling the number of observations minus 3. The t values, and their corresponding probability levels, can be interpreted as having the greatest likelihood of correspondence to the true t values for the obtained data given the estimated interdependence among the observations.

While this method adjusts the computed significance level for estimated interdependence, it does not completely remove the hazard of carry-over effects to a subsequent treatment phase, which may be enhanced or depressed by the influence of earlier treatment phases. It is also possible that the subsequent phase has no effect in its own right but that the preceding treatment phase does. If the effects of the preceding phase gradually fade out or extinguish during the course of administering the benign subsequent phase, the result may be misinterpreted as a progressively depressing influence attributable to the subsequent phase. Although a logical analysis of the nature of the respective treatment phases may obviate many of these problems, the investigator should be aware of their latent confounding influence and realize that complementary experimentation may be required in order to reduce these types of uncertainties.

An additional note of caution is in order. Typically, the investigator will wish to carry out several statistical tests if more than two treatment phases are incorporated into the design. In such cases, the independence (orthogonality) of these tests should be taken into consideration when interpreting the probability values provided by this procedure. For instance, the investigator may wish to detect any difference between a given treatment phase to an adjacent phase. This pattern of comparisons is depicted in the three contrasts under set 1 of Table 4-4. In this instance, the investigator is using a reversal or withdrawal type design of the *ABAB* variety. The coefficients, 1 and −1, signify which phases are involved in a given comparison, and the 0's indicate which ones are not. Two contrasts are independent only if the cross-products of their corresponding coefficients sum to 0. In the first set, contrasts 1 and 2 are nonorthogonal; so are contrasts 2 and 3; but contrasts 1 and 3 are orthogonal. Hence, set 1 consists of a nonorthogonal group of comparisons. However, sets 2 and 3 are orthogonal. If, as is usually the case, the investigator intends to make more than 2 specified pair-wise comparisons among the four treatment phases, the probability levels should be adjusted according to conventional methods for planned nonorthogonal comparisons (for example, Dunn's procedure) found in most standard research design texts. One straightforward method is to simply carry out each test at a

Table 4-4.
Illustrative Orthogonal and Nonorthogonal
Sets of Contrasts.

Treatment Phase	A	B	A	B
Set 1				
Contrast 1	1	−1	0	0
Contrast 2	0	1	−1	0
Contrast 3	0	0	1	−1
Set 2				
Contrast 1	1	−1	0	0
Contrast 2	0	0	1	−1
Set 3				
Contrast 1	1	0	−1	0
Contrast 2	0	1	0	−1

p value corresponding to some usual accepted significance level (.05) divided by the total number of comparisons carried out (.05/3 = .0167 for each comparison of set 1 in Table 4.4).

SIGNIFICANCE TESTING OF DISCREPANCIES IN SCORES FROM PSYCHOMETRIC TESTS

A common problem encountered by clinicians in the course of testing a treatment or theoretical hypothesis, or in the course of clinical assessment, is the discrepancy between two different tests administered to a single case. Interpretation of the discrepancy may be eigmatic depending on the size of the discrepancy and on the nature of the tests involved. For example, the clinician may wish to know the extent to which divergence of a patient's performance on tests of verbal and performance IQ reflects truly differing ability levels. If the divergence reflects a true difference in ability, how often is a difference of this size or larger found among the general population relevant to the present patient?

Discrepancy may also occur between results from two different occasions of administering the same test. For example, a clinical psychologist may be working with a physician on a spinal injury rehabilitation unit. The physician in charge suspects that a given treatment improves cognitive performance among his patients. Pre- and post-treatment measures of cognitive efficiency are available and the data indicates an apparent improvement. What is the likelihood of such improvement in the absence of intervention?

In the first instance, the clinician is asking, "Is the discrepancy between the two tests a *reliable* one?" In the second instance, the question is, "Given a reliable discrepancy, is it also an *abnormal* one?" The third instance involves a test of the null hypothesis that a change in test score over time can be attributed to sources of variance which are extraneous to the treatment intervention of interest. Payne and Jones[18] have presented some incisive statistical approaches to these questions. The statistical formulas and required data are given here; a more elaborate development of the computations are available from the earlier presentation by Payne and Jones.[18]

In each of the following tests, a Z value is derived. To assess the probability of a Z value at least as large as that obtained, given the null hypothesis, the user need only consult the normal-distribution table of an elementary statistics text. The following formula for Z is used to assess the null hypothesis that the discrepancy between scores from two tests X and Y is attributable to error of measurement:

$$Z = \frac{Z_x - Z_y}{[2 - (r_{xx} + r_{yy})]^{1/2}}$$

Here, r_{xx} is the coefficient of reliability for test X, r_{yy} is the coefficient of reliability for test Y,

$$Z_x = \frac{X - \bar{X}}{\sigma_x} \quad \text{and} \quad Z_y = \frac{Y - \bar{Y}}{\sigma_y}$$

where X is the patient's raw score on test X, $\bar{X}$ is the mean of all scores on test X among the referent population, and σ_x is the standard deviation of all scores on test X among the referent population. The terms Y, $\bar{Y}$ and σ_y are corresponding terms for test Y.

In order to obtain the Z value for testing the null hypothesis that a discrepancy between two test scores, X and Y, is a normal one, the following formula is used:

$$Z = \frac{Z_x - Z_y}{[2(1 - r_{xy})]^{1/2}}$$

The only new term is r_{xy}, the coefficient of correlation between test X and test Y.

The following formula is used for Z in order to test the null hypothesis that some treatment intervention has had no effect on a change in test score from time 1 (pretreatment) to time 2 (post-treatment):

$$Z = \frac{Y - Y'}{\sigma_y(1 - r_{xy}^2)^{1/2}}$$

Here, Y' is the value predicted from the linear regression equation,

$$a + bX;$$

$$b = r_{xy}\left(\frac{\sigma_y}{\sigma_x}\right) \quad \text{and} \quad a = \bar{Y} - b\bar{X}$$

The other terms are defined as follows:

$\bar{X}$ = The mean of all subjects in the referent population upon initial testing.

$\bar{Y}$ = The mean for all subjects in the referent population upon second testing.

σ_x = The referent population's standard deviation upon initial testing.

σ_y = The referent population's standard deviation upon second testing.

r_{xy} = Test-retest reliability with an intervening period approximately equal to that of the test-retest interval for the patient under consideration.

It should be noted that the referent population must not have had intervening treatment, as is usually the case for estimates of test-retest reliability.

The standard deviations, reliability coefficients, and inter-test correlations required for these formulas usually can be obtained from test manuals or reports in clinical journals.

DISCREPANCIES IN MEASURES AND PSYCHOMETRIC PROPERTIES OF TESTS

The first significance test of the preceding section dealt with the question of whether or not a divergence in test score results for a given subject was reliable—that is, it could not be reasonably attributed to errors of measurement alone. The question was approached by testing the significance of the obtained discrepancy using the available reliability coefficients for the two tests under consideration. Results of the significance test bear on the issue of the reliability of the obtained discrepancy in a particular instance. In a case where two tests are commonly used and discrepancies are often encountered, the clinician may wish to know if, in general, the tests measure identical or different traits or abilities. If there is complete overlap in the dimensions they measure, a discrepancy in a given instance is likely to reflect little more than test unreliability. If they measure different dimensions, the probability increases that a divergence in a particular case will reflect a genuine difference in some underlying trait or ability. Hence, the assessment of test score divergence in a given case can be aided by knowing whether the tests involved generally measure different dimensions over a large number of subjects.

Lord[14] has presented a statistical test, originally developed by Villegas,[20] designed to assess whether the tests under consideration measure a common dimension. If the statistical test is significant, the following null hypothesis can be rejected: Differences in the configurations of scores between two tests are attributable to errors of measurement, different units of measurement, and different arbitrary origins of measurement. Different units of measurement refer to inequalities in the way performance is quantified, such as using speed versus number of errors in intelligence subtests. Differing origins of measurement refer to inequalities in the meanings of different ranges of scores. For example, the maximum possible score on one arithmetic subtest may be an error rate of 30 percent while that for another subtest may be an error rate of 50 percent. Our main concern is usually with the effect of measurement errors since pairs of test scores usually have the same metric and origin or, if not, are referred to a common distribution as in the case of Z or T scores.

The significance test requires that each measure of the pair be administered more than once to each of a number of subjects. This requirement is most easily met when there are parallel forms of each test in the pair. In this case, there will be two administrations (or replicates) per subject. Let the measures be denoted g and h with x_{gnk} indicating the observation during the kth replicate (there being a total of r replicates) on the nth subject (there being a total of N subjects) for test g. The corresponding observation for test h is written as x_{hnk}.

Two 2 by 2 matrices, $\mathbf{W}$ and $\mathbf{A}$ must be formed. The first row and first column of each matrix correspond to test g and the second row and second column correspond to test h. The element of matrix $\mathbf{W}$ in row g and column g (see Appendix B) is obtained as follows:

$$w_{gg} = \sum_{n=1}^{N} \sum_{k=1}^{r} (x_{gnk} - \bar{x}_{gn.})^2$$

where $\bar{x}_{gn.}$ refers to the mean of the r replicates for test g and subject n. The value for the element in row h and column h is similarly computed using the scores for test h. The off-diagonal elements (see appendix B) are equal to each other and are computed as follows:

$$w_{gh} = w_{hg} = \sum_{n=1}^{N} \sum_{k=1}^{r} (x_{gnk} - \bar{x}_{gn.})(x_{hnk} - \bar{x}_{hn.})$$

The element in row g and column g of the matrix $\mathbf{A}$ is computed as follows:

$$a_{gg} = r \sum_{n=1}^{N} (\bar{x}_{gn.} - \bar{x}_{g..})^2$$

where $\bar{x}_{g..}$ refers to the grand mean of the scores on test g. The element a_{hh} is similarly computed using the scores for test h. The off-diagonal elements are computed as follows:

$$a_{gh} = a_{hg} = r \sum_{n=1}^{N} (\bar{x}_{gn.} - \bar{x}_{g..})(\bar{x}_{hn.} - \bar{x}_{h..})$$

Following the formation of matrix $\mathbf{W}$, each element is multiplied by a value from the F distribution. The F value is selected according to the adopted significance level (for example, p of .05) using N and $N(r - 1)$ degrees of freedom for the numerator and denominator, respectively. Let the resulting matrix be designated $\hat{\mathbf{W}}$. In addition, each element in the matrix $\mathbf{A}$ must be multiplied by $(r - 1)$ yielding the matrix $\hat{\mathbf{A}}$. A new matrix, $\mathbf{M}$ is then formed by subtracting $\hat{\mathbf{W}}$ from $\hat{\mathbf{A}}$; element m_{gh} of matrix $\mathbf{M}$ would be obtained as $(\hat{a}_{gh} - \hat{w}_{gh})$.

The last step in this test requires the calculation of the determinant of Matrix $\mathbf{M}$ (see Appendix B). In the case of a 2 by 2 matrix, this is easily arrived at by subtracting the product of the off-diagonal elements from that of the diagonal elements: $|\mathbf{M}| = (m_{gg})(m_{hh}) - (m_{gh})(m_{hg})$. If the determinant is positive, the null hypothesis—that configurations of scores between the two tests differ because of different units and origins of measurement and because of measurement error—is rejected at the selected p level. Rather, the hypothesis that they measure different systematic dimensions becomes tenable.

The assumptions required for valid use of the test surround the distribution of measurement errors—those components of test variation unrelated to the relatively enduring aspects of subject dispositions. The errors of measurement for the two tests can be correlated over subjects within a given replicate (for example, the first administration of the tests) and over replicates within a given subject. However, it is assumed that the correlation is zero for the errors within a given test between any two subjects over replicates, or between any two replicates over subjects. The latter implies that there are no practice effects over replicates. If practice effects exist, a conservative bias is introduced, meaning that the determinant $|\mathbf{M}|$ will sometimes be zero or negative when the null hypothesis should be rejected.

If the present test is significant, the clinician would conclude that the measures do not completely overlap in the traits or abilities tapped. Since the tests can potentially be affected by differences in systematic sources of variation, the clinician is more compelled to determine whether a discrepancy for a given patient is an instance of such a difference, versus an instance of the effects of test unreliability. The first significance test in the preceding section would be used to answer that question.

The test for complete overlap in measured dimensions can be illustrated with the following numerical example of hypothetical data. Suppose a clinician wishes to investigate a recurring discrepancy between scores on two measures of conceptual deficit in schizophrenia. Both measures are directed toward the ability to form abstract concepts. The first measure involves the interpretation of selected proverbs and the second measure requires the sorting of objects according to their common properties. The first test assesses abstracting ability with respect to verbal stimuli while the second test measures abstraction in relation to physical objects. A common problem with different measures of conceptual deficit is that they may reflect only a common dimension of general severity of deficit associated with overall degree of pathology, rather than the different aspects of conceptual deficit for which they were initially constructed.[2] If both tests measured only the dimension of deficit severity, discrepancies between them could generally be attributed to extraneous sources of variation including unreliability. The test for a common dimension of measurement could be used to deal with this issue. Suppose parallel forms of each test have been administered to 40 patients (thus, $N = 40$ and $r = 2$). The matrix W would then be computed and may appear as follows:

$$W = \begin{bmatrix} 160 & 100 \\ 100 & 150 \end{bmatrix}$$

Since the tabled value for F corresponding to $p = .05$ with 40, and 40 degrees of freedom is 1.69, the matrix $\hat{W}$ is:

$$\hat{W} = \begin{bmatrix} 270 & 169 \\ 169 & 254 \end{bmatrix}$$

The matrix A is equal to $\hat{A}$ because $r - 1$ is 1:

$$\hat{A} = \begin{bmatrix} 300 & 192 \\ 192 & 350 \end{bmatrix}$$

Finally, the matrix, M is the following:

$$M = \begin{bmatrix} 30 & 23 \\ 23 & 96 \end{bmatrix}$$

The determinant, $|\mathbf{M}|$, is $2880 - 529 = 2351$. As this value is positive, the null hypothesis—that there is complete overlap in the dimensions measured by the two tests—is rejected. The clinician may elect to retain both tests as measures of different components of conceptual deficit.

Although the preceding significance test has led to the conclusion that in general, different components of deficit are assessed by the two measures, a discrepancy obtained for a given patient may still not be due to a genuine difference in these components. It is possible that the measured components of deficit are equal for the particular patient and that the obtained divergence is attributable to errors of measurement. The clinician could then apply the first test of the preceding section to estimate the probability that the divergence arose from errors of measurement for a patient whose abilities tapped by the two tests are in fact equal.

REFERENCES

1. Appelbaum, M. I., & Cramer, E. M. Some problems in the nonorthogonal analysis of variance. *Psychol. Bull.*, 1974, **81**, 335–343.
2. Chapman, L. J., & Chapman, J. P. *Disordered thought in schizophrenia.* New York; Appleton-Century-Crofts, 1973.
3. Chassan, J. B. *Research design in clinical psychology and psychiatry.* New York; Appleton-Century-Crofts, 1967.
4. Cramer, E. M. *Revised MANOVA program.* Chapel Hill; University of North Carolina Psychometric Laboratory, 1967.
5. Davidson, P. O. Graduate training and research funding in clinical psychology in Canada. *Can. Psychol.*, 1971, **12**, 141–175.
6. Dixon, W. J. (Ed.). *BMD: Biomedical computer programs.* Los Angles; University of California Press, 1973.
7. Finn, J. *Multivariance: Univariate and multivariate analysis of variance, covariance, and regression (user's guide).* Ann Arbor; National Education Resources, Inc., 1972.
8. Glass, G. V., Wilson, V. K., & Gottman, J. M. *The design and analysis of time-series experiments.* Boulder, Col.: Laboratory of Educational Research Press, 1973.
9. Gottman, J. M. N of one and N of two research in psychotherapy. *Psychol. Bull.*, 1973, **80**, 93–105.
10. Gottman, J. M., McFall, R. M., & Barnett, J. T. Design and analysis of research using time series. *Psychol. Bull.*, 1969, **72**, 299–306.
11. Kirk, R. E. *Research design: Procedures for the behavioral sciences.* Belmont, Cal.: Brooks-Cole, 1968, p. 171.

12. Kirk, *Research design*, p. 455.
13. Leitenberg, H. The use of single-case methodology in psychotherapy research. *J. Abnorm. Psychol.*, 1973, **82**, 87–101.
14. Lord, F. M. Testing if two measuring procedures measure the same dimension. *Psychol. Bull.*, 1973, **79**, 71–72.
15. O'Brien, R. G. Comment on "Some problems in the nonorthogonal analysis of variance." *Psychol. Bull.*, 1976, **83**, 72–74.
16. Overall, J. E., & Klett, C. J. Applied Multivariate Analysis. New York McGraw-Hill, 1972, p. 441.
17. Overall, J. E., & Spiegel, D. K. Concerning least squares analysis of experimental data. *Psychol. Bull.*, 1969, **72**, 311–322.
18. Payne, R. W., & Jones, G. J. Statistics for the investigation of individual cases. *J. Clin. Psychol.*, 1957, **13**, 115–121.
19. Shapiro, M. B., Marks, I. M., & Fox, B. A therapeutic experiment on phobic and affective symptoms of an individual psychiatric patient. *Brit. J. Soc. Clin. Psychol.*, 1963, **2**, 81–93.
20. Villegas, C. Confidence region for a linear relation. *Ann. Math. Stat.* 1964, **35**, 780–788.
21. Winer, B. J. *Statistical principles in experimental design*. New York; McGraw-Hill, 1971. p. 752.

5

Quantifying Patterns of Symptom Change

A variety of methods are available for gleaning information from data other than those associated with statistical inference. However, quantitative methods not having some statement about the probability of the occurrence of the phenomenon of interest due to random sources (inferential statements) are often treated pejoratively. Typically, we think of descriptive quantification consisting of measures of the central tendency of a distribution such as the mean, median, or mode; and as some measure of dispersion such as the standard deviation. However, the more interesting and often more useful methods from the clinician's point of view are those which describe relations among variables. One of the features which makes the clinician's job so provocative and at the same time perplexing is the complex phenomena with which he is called upon to deal. As often as not, the difficulties presented by clients require one to take simultaneous account of a plethora of variables which may be in constant flux. The clinician must often attempt to gain an approximate picture of the interrelationship among the variables most salient to the immediate problem. Identification of the salient variables is largely a function of the clinician's amount of skill in applying extant research findings from the relevant disciplines and in capitalizing on past clinical experience. Familiarity with some of the relevant methods of analysis can greatly aid description of the interrelationships in quantitative terms.

UNCERTAINTY ANALYSIS

One of the problems often facing the clinician is that of quantifying relations among variables which are all categorial rather than
metrical. Categorical variables are those for which meaningful numerical values corresponding to changes are not forthcoming (such as the
designation of subjects as male or female).

If the predictor variables are metrical but the criterion is categorical, the method of choice for quantifying the relations between the
two sets of variables is discriminant-function analysis, described in
Chapter 6. However, often all variables germaine to the problem at
hand are categorical. Under these constraints, the method of choice
for quantifying the degree of relationship among the variables is
uncertainty analysis.[4,6,12]

Uncertainty analysis allows an estimate of the degree to which
the disposition of a patient on a categorical variable can be accounted
for by his position on one or more other categorical variables. In this
sense, uncertainty analysis refers to the extent to which uncertainty
about the first categorical variable can be reduced through knowledge
of the other categorical variable. The reduction in uncertainty of one
categorical variable through knowledge of the other parallels the
correlation between the two variables in the usual metric sense.
Where more than one categorical variable is relevant to the disposition on the other, the configuration is analogous to multiple correlation (discussed in Chapter 8). However, the more usual and preferred
analogy is factorial ANOVA,[5] since the total uncertainty reduced
through all the categorical predictors can be partitioned into components associated with each individual predictor—analogous to AN-
OVA main effects—and into a nonadditive component analogous to
the ANOVA interaction term.

Opportunities for this type of analysis are commonplace. Clinicians are often called upon to relate categories of prognosis such as
good, bad, or guarded, to categories of diagnosis. Categories of
preferred treatment programs such as chemotherapy or behavior
therapy are often related to categories of symptoms and/or signs,
specifically their presence or absence. In some instances, the clinician
may wish to treat metric data categorically if he suspects it of being
too "noisy" for fine shifts in metric values to reflect genuine
differences in patient status. At other times it may be pointless to
attempt to glean metric information from verbal reports made by
patients who can supply categorical information at best.

The statistic derived to quantify the degree of total uncertainty associated with a given categorical variable y was developed by Shannon[14] in 1949 and its use in a wide variety of situations for almost three decades has proven it to be markably robust. This statistic is:

$$U(y) = - \sum_{c=1}^{z} P(y_c) \, \mathrm{Log}_2 \, P(y_c)$$

It is assumed that there are z categories for variable y. The term $P(y_c)$ refers to the probability of an observation falling into the cth category from among the z available ones. The term $\mathrm{Log}_2 \, P(y_c)$ refers to the logarithm of the value $P(y_c)$ to the base 2. It is a simple matter to find the logarithm of this value to the more common base of 10 and then to multiply that logarithm by a factor of 3.32.

The approach taken to establishing the reduction in $U(y)$ is roundabout in the following sense (reference to Table 5-1 will help in following this discussion). The total initial uncertainty $U(y)$ is first

Table 5-1
Uncertainty-Analysis Computations for Fictitious Data: 1 Predictor Variable.

Predicted Variables (y)	Predictor Variable (x)			
	1	2	3	$\sum\limits_{q=1}^{p} x_q y_c$
1	33	3	2	38
2	10	20		30
3		5	27	32
$\sum\limits_{c=1}^{z} y_c x_q$	43	28	29	$\sum\limits_{q=1}^{p} \sum\limits_{c=1}^{z} x_q y_c = 100$

$$U(y) = - \sum_{c=1}^{z} P(y_c) \, \mathrm{Log}_2 \, P(y_c)$$
$$= -[.38(-1.395) + .30(-1.736) + .32(-1.643)] = 1.577$$
$$U_x(y) = - \sum_{q=1}^{p} \sum_{c=1}^{z} P(x_q) P(y_c | x_q) \, \mathrm{Log}_2 \, P(y_c | x_q)$$
$$= -[.43(33/43) \, \mathrm{Log}_2 \, (33/43) + .43(10/43) \, \mathrm{Log}_2 \, (10/43) + .28(3/28) \, \mathrm{Log}_2 \, (3/28) + .28(20/28) \, \mathrm{Log}_2 \, (20/28) + .28(5/28) \, \mathrm{Log}_2 \, (5/28) + .29(2/29) \, \mathrm{Log}_2 \, (2/29) + .29(27/29) \, \mathrm{Log}_2 \, (27/29)$$
$$= -[-.124 - .212 - .097 - .097 - .124 - .077 - .028] = .759$$
$$U(y:x) = U(y) - U_x(y) = 1.577 - .759 = .818$$

Note: The negative signs preceding the computational formulas can be ignored if those of the logarithms are also ignored.

calculated. Then the residual uncertainty, which remains after the predictor variable (denoted x) is known, is computed. The residual uncertainty is denoted $U_x(y)$. It follows that the reduction in uncertainty available from knowing the categorical value of x can be obtained as:

$$U(y:x) = U(y) - U_x(y)$$

The value for $U_x(y)$ is calculated as:

$$U_x(y) = - \sum_{q=1}^{p} \sum_{c=1}^{z} p(x_q) P(y_c|x_q) \text{Log}_2 P(y_c|x_q)$$

The term $P(y_c|x_q)$ refers to the probability of y_c given the qth category of x and is considered the *contingent probability* of y_c under condition x_q.

The probability values are taken as proportions of observations falling into the designated categories. For example, $P(x_q)$ is the total number of observations falling into the qth category of x divided by the total number of observations in all categories of x (Table 5-1). Contingent probabilities are similarly calculated, except that the number of observations are based on the designated category *combinations*. For example, $P(y_c|x_q)$ would be obtained as the number of observations in the cth category of y and the qth category of x, divided by the total number of observations in the qth category of x.

Uncertainty analysis accomodates more than two variables at a time. This feature is particularly advantageous because the variable of interest, such as amenability to a given treatment procedure, may be related to multiple categorical predictors consisting of several symptom-sign categories.

In order to carry out a thorough analysis with more than one predictor, the uncertainty reduction associated with each predictor must be calculated individually (analagous to computing main effects in ANOVA), along with the uncertainty reduction that remains after the reduction associated with the individual variables has been removed. The remaining uncertainty reduction is considered the nonadditive effects of the individual variables and is analogous to the interaction term in ANOVA.

In the three-variable situation, where x and w represent the predictor variables, the reductions in uncertainty associated with x, w and $x \times w$ nonadditivity or "interaction" are denoted $U(y:x)$, $U(y:w)$ and $U(\overline{wxy})$, respectively. To facilitate computations, a three-mode data matrix is required, as depicted in Table 5-2. A pair of two-mode matrices can in turn be constructed from the data in the three-mode matrix. The values $U(y:x)$ and $U(y:w)$ can be calculated from the corresponding two-mode matrices with the same procedures that were used in the single-predictor situation presented in Table 5-1. The residual uncertainty remaining after predictability from variables x, w and their nonadditivity has been exhausted is denoted $U_{xw}(y)$, and its computation can be easily extrapolated from the computation of

Table 5-2
Illustrative Uncertainty Analysis for Two Predictor Variables.

		w_1		w_2	
		x_1	x_2	x_1	x_2
y_1		30	5	40	20
y_2		5	60	30	10

	x_1	x_2	$\sum\limits_{q=1}^{p} x_q y_c$
y_1	70	25	95
y_2	35	70	105
$\sum\limits_{c=1}^{z} y_c x_q$	105	95	$\sum\limits_{q=1}^{p}\sum\limits_{c=1}^{z} x_q y_c = 200$

$$\left(x_q y_c = \sum_{i=1}^{n} w_i x_q y_c\right)$$

	w_1	w_2	$\sum\limits_{i=1}^{n} w_i y_c$
y_1	35	60	95
y_2	65	40	105
$\sum\limits_{c=1}^{z} y_c w_i$	100	100	

$$\left(w_i y_c = \sum_{q=1}^{p} x_q w_i y_c\right)$$

$$U(y) = -\sum_{c=1}^{z} P(y_c)\,\mathrm{Log}_2\,P(y_c) = -[.475(-1.07) + .525(-.93)] = .996$$

$$U(y:x) = U(y) - U_x(y)$$

$$U_x(y) = -\sum_{q=1}^{p}\sum_{c=1}^{z} P(x_q)P(y_c|x_q)\,\mathrm{Log}_2\,P(y_c|x_q)$$

e.g., $P(x_1)P(y_1|x_1)\,\mathrm{Log}_2\,P(y_1|x_1) = (105/200)(70/105)(-.577) = -.202$

$$U(y:w) = U(y) - U_w(y)$$

$$U_w(y) = -\sum_{i=1}^{n}\sum_{c=1}^{z} P(w_i)P(y_c|w_i)\,\mathrm{Log}_2\,P(y_c|w_i)$$

e.g., $P(w_1)P(y_1|w_1)\,\mathrm{Log}_2\,P(y_1|w_1) = (100/200)(35/100)(-1.514) = -.265$

$$U(\overline{wxy}) = U(y) - U_{wx}(y) - U(y:x) - U(y:w)$$

$$U_{wx}(y) = \sum_{q=1}^{p}\sum_{i=1}^{n}\sum_{c=1}^{z} P(x_q w_i)P(y_c|x_q w_i)\,\mathrm{Log}_2\,P(y_c|x_q w_i)$$

e.g., $P(x_1 w_1)P(y_1|x_1 w_1)\,\mathrm{Log}_2\,P(y_1|x_1 w_1) = (35/200)(30/35)(-.217) = -.032$

$U_x(y)$ in Table 5-1. Table 5-2 presents the computational formulas for this analysis along with illustrations of the terms used in the formulas.

The formula for the term $U(\overline{wxy})$ can be treated from an ANOVA viewpoint in the following manner. The total variance in a two-factor experiment can be partitioned into four sources: the two main effects, the interaction, and experimental error, corresponding to $U_{xw}(y)$. Thus, the interaction can be estimated by subtracting the two main effects and the experimental error from the total.

Illustration of Uncertainty Analysis of Clinical Data

Metcalfe[10] reported data from an experimental study of a 21-year-old female asthmatic. It was suspected that her asthma attacks were exacerbated by emotional stimulation, specifically that associated with contact with her mother. Metcalfe tabulated the relationship between asthma onset within 24 hours of maternal contact. The pattern of results is presented in Table 5-3(a).

In addition to maternal contact, it was suspected that the home environment of the patient contributed to the attacks. Data relevant to this hypothesis are listed in Table 5-3(b). Metcalfe applied a χ^2 contingency test to each set of data and reported that the relationship represented by Table 5-3(a) was significant beyond the .01 level while that of Table 5-3(b) was not quite significant at the .05 level.

The additional information provided by uncertainty analysis can be illustrated in this example. The absolute uncertainty reduction provided by knowledge of the mother's presence or absence was .079 "bits" ("bits" is the usual designation for units of uncertainty)—that provided by knowledge of whether or not maternal contact occurred in the home was .10 bits. Hence, the magnitudes of uncertainty reduction were in the opposite direction of the significance levels of the χ^2 contingency tests. One of the reasons for this result may have been that the absolute amount of uncertainty about an attack ab initio was relatively low because of the high base-rate of no-attack days according to Table 5-3(a). Conversely, in the second analysis the initial uncertainty of y was comparatively higher. This illustration points up the importance of considering the entire configuration of information available in matrices of this type of clinical data: the statistical significance of relationships; their absolute size; and finally the uncertainty about the occurrence of the predicted variable prior to the introduction of the predictor.

Table 5-3
Use of Uncertainty Analysis on Clinical Data.

(a)

	x_1 (mother present)	x_2 (mother absent)	$\sum\limits_{q=1}^{p} x_q y_c$
y_1 (asthma onset)	9	6	15
y_2 (no asthma onset)	14	56	70
$\sum\limits_{c=1}^{z} y_c x_q$	23	62	$\sum\limits_{q=1}^{p}\sum\limits_{c=1}^{z} x_q y_c = 85$

$$U(y) = -\sum_{c=1}^{z} P(y_c)\, \mathrm{Log}_2\, P(y_c) = .679$$

$$U_x(y) = -\sum_{q=1}^{p}\sum_{c=1}^{z} P(x_q)P(y_c \mid x_q)\, \mathrm{Log}_2\, P(y_c \mid x_q) = -[.27(.39)(-1.36) +$$

$$.27(.61)(-.71) + .73(.10)(-3.32) + .73(.90)(-.15)] = .600$$

$$U(y{:}x) = .679 - .600 = .079$$

(b)

	x_1 (at home)	x_2 (not at home)	$\sum\limits_{q=1}^{p} x_q y_c$
y_1 (asthma onset)	7	2	9
y_2 (no asthma onset)	5	9	14
$\sum\limits_{c=1}^{z} y_c x_q$	12	11	23

$$U(y) = .96$$
$$U_x(y) = .86$$
$$U(y{:}x) = .96 - .86 = .10$$

STOCHASTIC PROCESS ANALYSIS

Like uncertainty analysis, stochastic process analysis is concerned with categorical relations. It is addressed specifically to the *sequential* relations among a designated set of categories and represents a method of describing the likelihood that one categorical event will follow another. In that sense, it is concerned with "chains" of events as they occur over time. Using the preceding example to illustrate, suppose that our concern this time is not whether the patient's asthmatic attacks follow maternal contact, but if a day with an attack is followed by a day with another attack versus an attack-free day.

The basic datum of our analysis is the probability of an event following another event. The first event is termed an antecedent and the event which follows it a consequent. The type of sequence on which the probability values are based is called a Markov chain. It should be noted that the antecedent and the consequent can refer to the same event (as in the example, days with asthmatic attacks).

Extensive treatments of Markovian analysis have been available for some time[9] but this method has been used quite sparingly in the clinical setting. Hertel[7] has presented the method to clinicians as a potentially useful tool for describing sequences of behavioral events in psychotherapy. The method appears to be useful for a variety of situations in which the clinician is concerned with the quantitative description of any sequential process having definable categories.

The sequence of events associated with recidivism among alcoholics may be amenable to this type of analysis. The alcoholic patient may engage in binge behavior, followed by a drying-out period in an institution, followed in turn by gainful employment, which may again be followed by binge behavior. Alternatively the drying-out period may be followed by more binge behavior, or the gainful employment followed by seeking support from other patients with arrested alcoholism, leading subsequently to extended abstinence, and so on. Identifying the probabilities of the events in sequence among a large sample of alcoholic patients and submitting the data to stochastic-process analysis may provide valuable information about the pattern of recidivism. This data may in turn be used to suggest hypotheses about times when therapeutic intervention would yield best results.

Stochastic-process analysis also appears to bear imminent relevance to the type of information clinicians consider important in behavior therapy. This information consists of the probability that a given behavioral event, such as diminished social activity, will follow certain antecedent conditions, such as being rebuffed by a friend.[11]

Computing the probabilities of consequent events following antecedent events is a relatively simple matter. One need only keep track of the sequence of events over an extended period and compute the proportion of times each antecedent was followed by each consequent.

Consider the two-category situation of the presence versus absence of an asthmatic attack during a 24-hour period, designated *a* and *b* respectively. Let the sequence of events sampled from an abbreviated period of time be as follows:

$$a \to a \to b \to a \to b \to b \to b \to a \to b \to b \to a \to a \to b$$

where $\to$ denotes transition from antecedent to consequent.

In this instance *a* occurs as an antecedent six times, followed by itself twice, and by *b* four times. The probability of $a \to a$ is 2/6 = .33. The probability of $a \to b$ is 4/6 = .67. Similarly, the probability of $b \to a$ is 3/6 = .5 and the probability of $b \to b$ is .5. These computations represent the probabilities of the respective consequents after a single transition to the immediately following events, and are arranged accordingly in the first-order matrix of Table 5-4. The specific event occurring after several transitions is likely to be of additional interest to the clinician. The chains represented in Figure 5-1 present the events occurring after two transitions and the sequences by which they emerged, following antecedents *a* and *b*. The right-hand column indicates the probabilities of each consequent for each sequential path. As shown in Figure 5-1, these probabilities can be calculated using the single-transition values listed in the first-order matrix. The probability of a given state after two transitions under each antecedent can be obtained by summing the probabilities of the sequential paths yielding the state. For example, the probability of obtaining *a* upon the second transition, given *a* as an antecedent, is .11 + .33 = .44. The probability of obtaining state *a* upon two transitions with *b* as an antecedent is .16 + .25 = .41. More conveniently, these probabilities can be obtained by squaring the first-order matrix—that is, by multiplying it by itself (see Appendix B)—leading to the second-order matrix of Table 5-4. For instance, the element in the first row and second column of the second-order matrix is equal to (.33)(.66) + (.66)(.50) = .55. Similarly, the probabilities of each category after any

Table 5-4
First- and Second-Order Contingency Matrices.

| | First-Order Matrix Consequent | | | Second-Order Matrix Consequent | |
	a	*b*		*a*	*b*
Antecedent			*Antecedent*		
a	.33	.66	*a*	.44	.55
b	.50	.50	*b*	.41	.58

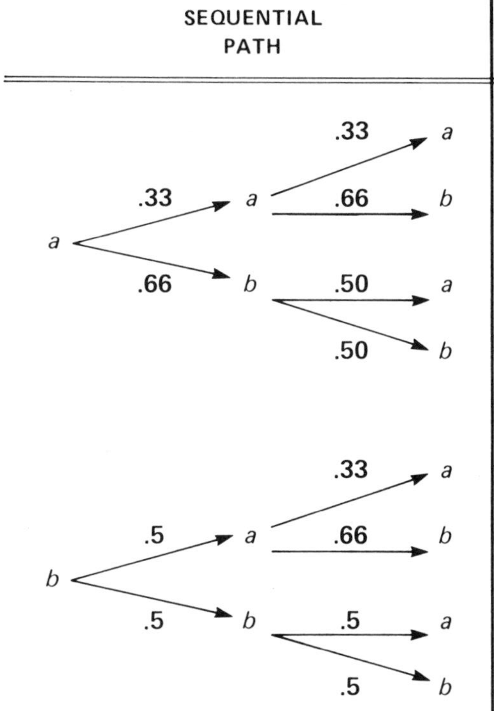

SEQUENTIAL PATH	PROBABILITY OF EACH SEQUENTIAL PATH	
	$.33 \times .33 = .11$	Probability of moving from a to a in 2 transitions $= .11 + .33 = .44$
	$.33 \times .66 = .22$	
	$.66 \times .50 = .33$	Probability of moving from a to b in 2 transitions $= .22 + .33 = .55$
	$.66 \times .50 = .33$	
	$.5 \times .33 = .16$	Probability of moving from b to a in 2 transitions $= .16 + .25 = .41$
	$.5 \times .66 = .33$	
	$.5 \times .5 = .25$	Probability of moving from b to b in 2 transitions $= .33 + .25 = .58$
	$.5 \times .5 = .25$	

Fig. 5-1. Hypothetical two-category chain with two transitions.

number of transitions in the process can be obtained by taking the first-order matrix to the power of that number. In the present example, the third-order matrix could be obtained by cubing the first order matrix of Table 5-4.

It is apparent that the probability values dealt with up to now are contingent probability values. They are the probabilities of the consequents, given the respective antecedents. The noncontingent probabilities are also available. These values correspond to the probabilities of the consequents with the antecedents unspecified. The noncontingent probabilities can be obtained simply by multiplying the rows of the various-order matrices by the initial probabilities of the corresponding antecedents. In the asthma attack example, the initial probabilities of a and of b were quite similar according to their relative frequencies of occurrence in the sequence (6 for a and 7 for b). Thus, each value in row a would be multiplied by .46 and each value in row b would be multiplied by .54.

The categorical events described in these analyses are mutually exclusive; only one event at a time can occur as an antecedent or as a consequent. In the asthma example, the patient could not have both an asthma attack and no asthma attack on the same day. However, she could have an attack or not have an attack in combination with visiting her mother. Hence, the three-category set of asthma attack onset (a), no asthma attack onset (b), and maternal contact (c), would not be mutually exclusive and therefore not amenable to this analysis as it has been outlined here.

Stochastic processes can be described by several types of patterns. Hertel[7] has discussed the main patterns in detail along with their implications for psychotherapy research. A number of available statistics, including the mean and variance of the probability values in the various-order matrices and the likelihood that a given event will be included among the transitions mediating the passage from one event to another, along with significance tests for differences in these indices between various matrices, are available[9], and appear to have potential utility in the clinical setting.

When similar stochastic-process analyses are applied to a number of subjects, the raw probability values can be averaged and/or submitted to analysis of variance. For example, an investigator may obtain the probabilities of three consequents associated with a particular antecedent after the first, second, and third transitions. These probabilities could be submitted to an analysis of variance with the three consequents and the three transitions each forming a within-subject three-level factor.

We can conclude that stochastic process analysis has the potential of being a very useful clinical tool. With some ingenuity, there is little doubt that it provides increased precision for describing a variety of clinical processes whose contingent events are categorically designated.

AUTOCORRELATION AS A SOURCE OF CLINICAL INFORMATION: THE USE OF CORRELOGRAMS

The autocorrelation effect (described in Chapters 2 and 4) has been troublesome to clinicians attempting to assess the statistical significance of treatment differences on individual subjects, but also an informational asset to those who consider cyclical changes over time to be important content in the overall clinical picture of the patient. The autocorrelation effect can be estimated using lag correlations described below, which can be plotted in the form of correlograms.[8] Like stochastic-process analysis, autocorrelation analysis addresses patterns of relations over time. In stochastic-process analysis, we are concerned about the probabilities of certain categorical events following other categorical events over several numbers of transitions. Autocorrelation analysis pertains to the degree of predictability of one metrical (or interval) observation from another as a function of the time separating the observations.

Computing the lag correlation employs the formula for Pearson's r. The pairs of observations entering into the computations are formed on the basis of separation in time according to the designated time lag. In the usual application of Pearson's r, the correlation between two measures such as age and intelligence is computed across N subjects, there being one pair of scores (one for each measure) per subject. A lag correlation, however, is computed between a given time interval across those pairs of data points separated by the given interval. In the former case, the value of r would indicate the degree of correspondence between the two measures; in the latter case, it would indicate the degree of correspondence between observations taken at one point in time and those occurring at the designated time period later.

For example, let 100 observations be obtained at weekly intervals. The lag correlation between a one-week interval, called lag-1, would be computed using the data points separated by one week. In this case, the computation would involve pairs of observations corresponding to weeks one and two, weeks two and three, weeks

three and four, and so on up to weeks 99 and 100. In general, where
the data points are separated by the designated interval of l (the lag-l
correlation), the computational formula to be used is:

$$(1/N - l) \sum_{i=1}^{N-l} \frac{x_i - \bar{x}_{(1; N - l)}}{\sigma_{(1; N-l)}} \frac{x_{i+l} - \bar{x}_{(l; N)}}{\sigma_{(l; N)}}$$

where x_i and x_{i+l} are the raw score values for the dependent
   variable on occasions i and $i + l$, respectively;
$\bar{x}_{(1; N-l)}$ and $\sigma_{(1; N-l)}$ are the mean and standard deviation,
   respectively, for the first $N - l$ observations;
and $\bar{x}_{(l; N)}$ and $\sigma_{(l; N)}$ are the mean and standard deviation,
   respectively, for the last $N - l$ observations.

The meaning of differing sizes of lag correlations can be illustrated using a graphical representation of cyclical data. In Figure 5-2
the segment of data represents a pattern which would yield correlations of differing sizes, depending on the degree of lag. For example,
lag-1 correlation would be expected to be large and positive since, in
general, as each data point increases or decreases, so does the point
immediately following. The expected correlations for lags greater than

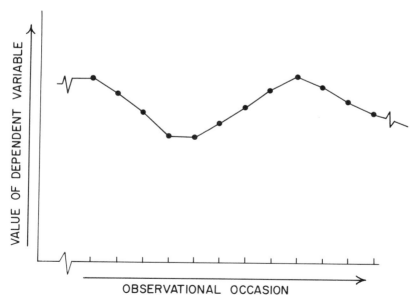

Fig. 5-2.   Illustrative segment of scores for hypothetical lag correlation.

1 can be verified with the pairs of observations entering into the corresponding computations. As the lag proceeds from 1 through about 4, the relatively large positive correlation would be expected to become relatively large and negative; as the lag proceeds from 4 through 8, the correlation would be expected to change back to relatively large and positive.

With cyclical data such as that of Figure 5-2, the autocorrelation effect acquires an important property: The correlation among observations increases and decreases at regular, temporal intervals. In Chapters 2 and 4, the autocorrelation effect resulted from higher correlations among temporally proximal observations relative to temporally distant observations. In the present context, such a configuration would correspond to decreasing magnitudes of correlations with increasing lag size. This principle usually holds with noncyclical data,[2,13] unlike cyclical data where the maximum correlation is determined by the lag interval of the cycle. The pattern in the segment of Figure 5-2 suggests a maximum positive correlation between those observations separated by a lag of 8.

An approximate test of the statistical significance of a lag correlation can be made by calculating the usual test for Pearson's r or, more conveniently, by using a table of significant values of r corresponding to various degrees of freedom.[1] Typically the significance of each lag correlation from the whole set of lag correlations is ascertained. The obtained significance levels should be treated as little more than descriptions of the correlations. The descriptive approach to a significant correlation specifically adopts the orientation, "If this were the only correlation computed in this study and if the significance test were exact rather than approximate, a correlation of this size or higher would occur no more than one time in 20 (given an adopted p level of .05) if the population correlation were in fact 0." The lag correlation values attaining this type of descriptive significance can give a better picture of the cyclical pattern of the data. Note that the relevant number of degrees of freedom are based on the number of pairs of values participating in the computation (specifically $N - 1 - 2$); therefore, as the lag size increases, so does the absolute value of the correlation required to attain significance.

The partial correlation coefficient can be used in addition to the application of the usual correlation coefficient to lagged data. Use of partial correlation allows an estimate of that correlation remaining over a lag of a given size when the one associated with a lag of a different size is partialled out.[8] Partial correlation can be used to estimate the amount of lag or distance between observations required before the relationship between the observations becomes negligible.

For example, the formula for the lag-2 correlation with predictable variance from lag-1 partialled out is:

$$r_{2.1} = \frac{r_2 - r_1{}^2}{1 - r_1{}^2}$$

where r_1 and r_2 refer to the lag-1 and lag-2 correlations, respectively.

Example of the Use of Correlograms in Describing Cyclical Clinical Data

Stenn and Klinge[15] measured the basal body temperature of several male and female subjects over an extended period of time. They computed correlations of various lags in an effort to compare changes in basal temperature as a function of the menstrual cycle. The lag correlation values for a representative female subject are presented in the form of a correlogram in Figure 5-3. Those for a representative male are presented in the correlogram of Figure 5-4.

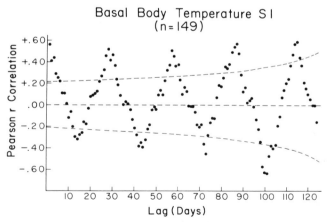

Fig. 5-3. Lag correlogram of basal body temperature in a female subject. (From "Relationship between menstrual cycle and bodily activity in humans" by P. G. Stenn and V. Klinge, *Hormones and Behavior*, 1973, **3**, 297–305. Copyright 1973 by Academic Press, Reprinted by permission.)

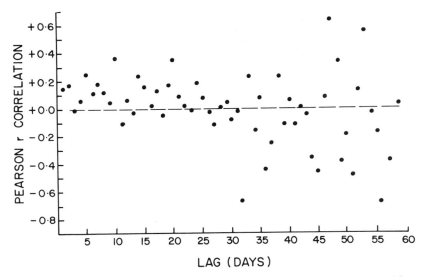

Fig. 5-4. Lag correlogram of basal body temperature in a male subject. (From "Relationship between menstrual cycle and bodily activity in humans" by P. G. Stenn and V. Klinge, *Hormones and Behavior*, 1973, *3*, 297–305. Copyright 1973 by Academic Press. Reprinted by permission.)

The upper and lower hatched lines in Figure 5-3 represent values of Pearson's correlation coefficient that correspond to significance at the .01 level, given the degrees of freedom for the various lag values. These figures evidence a salient influence of the menstrual cycle on basal body temperature. Cyclical patterns in nonphysiological dependent variables may be less pronounced. In any case, this example illustrates the potential sensitivity of lag-correlation analysis to cyclical trends in (real) clinical data.

CONCLUDING COMMENTS

This chapter has by no means exhausted the battery of methods available for describing patterns of variation in symptomatology. The methods here were selected because they are less familiar to clinicians than are a number of other available approaches, and because they are relatively versatile due to their applicability to symptom-related data obtained by a wide range of means. Other methods have been presented in a volume of readings by Davidson and Costello.[3]

Quantitative methods useful to clinicians are available for many problems other than those associated with patient-specific symptom changes. These methods relate to problems at the institutional level as well as to clinically relevant information from group data. They include both multivariate procedures (Chapters 8 through 10) and univariate methods (Chapters 6 and 7).

REFERENCES

1. Baggaley, A. *Intermediate correlation methods.* New York; Wiley, 1964.
2. Box, G. E. Some theorems on quadratic forms: II. Effect of inequality of variance and of correlation of errors in the two-way classification. *Annals. Math. Stat.,* 1954, **25,** 484–498.
3. Davidson, P. O., & Costello, C. G. $N = 1$: *Experimental studies of single cases.* New York: Van Nostrand, 1969.
4. Garner, W. R. *Uncertainty and structure as psychological concepts.* New York: Wiley, 1962.
5. Garner, W. R., & McGill, W. J. The relation between information and variance analysis. *Psychometrika.,* 1956, **21,** 219–229.
6. Hake, H. W., & Rodwan, A. S. Perception and recognition. In J. Sidowski (Ed.), *Experimental methods and instrumentation in psychology.* New York: McGraw-Hill, 1966, p. 331.
7. Hertel, R. K. Application of stochastic process analyses to the study of psychotherapeutic processes. *Psychol. Bull.,* 1972, **77,** 421–430.
8. Holtzman, W. H. Statistical models for the study of change in the single case. In C. Harris (Ed.), *Problems in measuring change.* Madison, Wis.: University of Wisconsin Press, 1963, p. 199.
9. Kemeny, J. G., & Snell, J. L. *Finite markov chains.* New York: Van Nostrand, 1960.
10. Metcalfe, M. Demonstration of a psychosomatic relationship. *Br. J. Med. Psychol.,* 1956, **29,** 63–66.
11. Rimm, D. C., & Masters, J. C. Behavior therapy: Techniques and empirical findings. New York: Academic Press, 1974, p. 34.
12. Rozeboom, W. W. *Foundations of the theory of prediction.* Homewood, Ill.: Dorsey Press, 1966, p. 565.
13. Scheffé, H. *The analysis of variance.* New York: Wiley, 1959, p. 331.
14. Shannon, C. E. *The mathematical theory of communication.* Urbana, Ill.: University of Illinois Press, 1949.
15. Stenn, P. G., & Klinge, V. Relationship between the menstrual cycle and bodily activity in humans. *Horm. Beh.,* 1973, **3,** 297–305.

6

Some Methods Facilitating Decision Making in Clinical Practice

INTRODUCTION

One of the tasks increasingly assigned to clinicians, especially those in institutional settings, is to evaluate the adequacy of ongoing programs in meeting stated goals. The evaluation centers around the utility of ongoing assessment procedures, the relative costs of different kinds of decision errors surrounding patient classification or revision of some treatment procedure, and the cost versus the accrued benefit resulting from the institution of some administrative innovation in the institution.

The methods used in making evaluations center on two aspects of the decisional context. One is the comparative probabilities of the outcomes of concern, and the other is the value—utility or cost—associated with these outcomes. Where primary interest centers only on the probabilities of certain outcomes, decisions may be made using that information with no formal calculation of the costs or utilities involved. In other cases, the costs and utilities may be specified and included in formal calculations.

BAYES' THEOREM AND THE PROBABILITY OF OUTCOMES

Prediction is one of the major challenges recurrently facing the clinician. This challenge can be stated in general terms as the task of making some statement about a state of affairs of clinical interest. The state of affairs may refer to a future event such as the probability that a given course of action will yield to clients benefits which outweigh the cost of the action to the institution. The state of affairs may also refer to more conclusive information about some extant event such as whether or not a patient has damage to some part of the left brain hemisphere.

In the enterprise of prediction, the clinician can take whatever he suspects to be available evidence that relates to the state of affairs to be predicted, and make some estimate of that state. Chapter 8 deals with methods for mathematically combining several sources of evidence in order to arrive at a best estimate of a patient's score on the predicted variable (multiple regression) or, alternately, for arriving at a best estimate of some category (such as diagnostic) to which the patient belongs (discrimination-function analysis).

The clinician may also wish to use a piece of evidence in order to make statements about the probabilities of alternative events.* The basic tool typically used in developing this type of statements is known as Bayes' Theorem. In presenting this theorem, the alternative outcome events will be designated $O_c(c = 1, 2, \ldots, z)$. Thus, there are z outcomes or events about which probability statements are to be made. In the common case of two events, such as whether or not a patient has an IQ above 100, $z = 2$. The categories of evidence which bear on this query are denoted $E_q(q = 1, 2, \ldots, p)$. The theorem is written as follows:

(1)
$$P(O_{c'}/E_{q'}) = \frac{P(E_{q'}/O_{c'})P(O_{c'})}{\sum\limits_{c=1}^{z} P(E_{q'}/O_c)P(O_c)}$$

where $P(O_{c'}/E_{q'})$ is the probability that the specific event $O_{c'}$ is the existing state of affairs when the category of evidence $E_{q'}$ has emerged;

$P(E_{q'}/O_{c'})$ is the probability that the category of evidence $E_{q'}$ will emerge when the specific event $O_{c'}$ prevails;

and $P(O_{c'})$ is the "unconditional" probability of specific event $O_{c'}$.

The unconditional probability of $O_{c'}$ is interpreted as the proportion of

---

* It should be mentioned that discriminant-function analysis can result in statements about the relative probabilities of group membership rather than in just a statement consisting of the single category to which the patient belongs based on a computed best estimate.[2]

all z events which consist of the specific event $O_{c'}$, temporarily ignoring the obtained evidence. The denominator of the ratio above is simply the probabilities of the obtained evidence $E_{q'}$ under conditions of event O_c, times the unconditional probability of O_c, summed across all z events O_c.

Suppose a patient is suspected of having damage to some part of the left brain hemisphere and is referred to a neuropsychologist for further testing. For the present purpose, let the outcome events be either the presence or absence of the suspected damage with O_1 denoting its presence, and O_2 denoting its absence. Let the evidence $E_{q'}$ be the presence of a given type of speech impairment displayed by the patient. The clinician can now make use of data from hospital files which bear on his problem. Suppose the files indicate that, according to subsequent testing of patients previously referred by this physician under similar circumstances, the proportion who have actually possessed the suspected damage has been .40. Given this data, $P(O_1)$ is .40 and $P(O_2)$ is $1 - .40$, or .60. The files also indicate that of those patients having the suspected damage, 70 percent have displayed the same kind of speech anomaly as the present patient. Of those without the damage, 10 percent have displayed the anomaly. Thus, $P(E_{q'}/O_1)$ is .70 and $P(E_{q'}/O_2)$ is .10. Using Bayes' theorem, the probability that this patient has damage to his left brain hemisphere, given the present impairment, can be assessed as:

$$P(O_1/E_{q'}) = \frac{(.70 \times .40)}{(.70 \times .40) + (.10 \times .60)} = .82$$

The probability that the patient does not have the damage, given the impairment, is:

$$P(O_2/E_{q'}) = \frac{(.10 \times .60)}{(.70 \times .40) + (.10 \times .60)} = .18$$

This example shows how our change in beliefs about the relative probabilities of the alternative events, given the evidence at hand, can be quantified using Bayes' theorem. Specifically, our beliefs about the presence of the damage prior to the obtained evidence of impairment is represented by a probability value of .40. In Baysian terminology, the value of $P(O_1)$ is referred to as the *prior* probability of O_1. Our beliefs about the presence of damage following the evidence of impairment have changed to a probability value of .82. This value of $P(O_1/E_{q'})$ is referred to as the *posterior* probability of O_1. The term which is relevant to our change in beliefs, $P(E_{q'}/O_1)$, is designated the *likelihood function*. A comparison of the posterior probabilities of O_1 and O_2 indicates that the probability of the presence of damage is 4.55 times that of the absence of damage: This ratio of probabilities is known as the *posterior odds ratio*.

Because the clinician's findings are so often translated into a description of the probabilities of relevant outcomes, this type of Baysian computation can contribute to an assessment problem with great advantage. In these circumstances, the referring clinician is likely to take the information and incorporate it formally or informally into a decision-making process regarding a course of action for the patient. The assessing clinician has done his job in specifying the relevant probabilities as precisely as possible. The use of this information in deciding what is to be done for the patient is a policy decision residing with the initially referring clinician.

However, the more typical clinical problem does not stop with a description of the status of various outcomes in terms of probability. Instead, decisions must be made which in turn carry the possibility of errors. Actions resulting from erroneous decisions can be costly. The cost can range from loss of life due to a false conclusion such as, "Patient X will not commit suicide during a weekend leave," to the rather mild cost of prescribing injected versus oral phenothiazine for a patient who has a fear of syringes. The following extension of Baysian analysis is directed toward situations where courses of action based on the computational results must be taken. The goal of this extension is to avoid those decisional actions which are most costly.

Baysian Analyses as Applied to Costs of Different Outcomes

In the numerical example of the preceding section, the posterior probability of one of the two alternative outcomes was 4.55 times that of the other (corresponding to comparative posterior probabilities of .82 versus .18). A decision about patient status based on this evidence would be one favoring the outcome associated with the probability value of .82. In the example, that outcome was that the patient was brain damaged in some part of the left hemisphere. Hence, the patient would be diagnosed as having the suspected damage and followed up by an appropriate treatment procedure. Note the risk that this course of action may be wrong. Specifically, the posterior probability that the patient does not have the suspected brain damage is .18—the probability of incorrectly treating the patient as though the suspected brain damage existed. The cost of so treating the patient might be available and, if so, its quantity times the probability of the error yields the *expected cost* of treating a given patient as though he were suffering the suspected brain damage.

Correspondingly, the expected cost of erroneously treating the patient as though he were not brain damaged, when in fact he was, would be obtained as the product of the cost of such a miscalculation times .82. The value of .82 refers to the probability of error under a negative decision regarding the issue of brain damage. If the cost of the first error—treating a patient without damage as though there were damage—were sufficiently high (as in the case of unnecessary surgery), the decision might be in favor of treating the patient as though there were no damage, even though the posterior odds ratio favored the presence of damage by a factor of 4.55.

Suppose that each type of error referred to could be scaled on a continuum reflecting arbitrary quantities of cost. Suppose further that the cost of treating a patient without the suspected damage as though he had the damage was ten times the cost of treating a patient with the suspected damage as though it were absent. The posterior odds ratio times the cost ratio would be less than 1, $(.82/.18)(1/10) = .455$, implying that the first error would be more costly to make than the second.

Perhaps the greatest difficulty in implementing expected cost analyses in the clinical setting consists of quantifying the costs associated with the varous types of errors into comparable units. Alternative approaches to this problem are discussed later in this chapter, in the section on estimates of cost and utility.

THE RELATIVE UTILITIES OF TREATMENT VERSUS NO TREATMENT

An issue that often plagues members of a clinical staff is whether or not to administer a given treatment to a patient, or in some cases, whether to treat the patient at all. In many cases, the individual may deny the need for treatment and the question arises of admitting him to an institution on an involuntary basis. If the individual requires treatment but it is not given, the presenting symptoms may intensify. On the other hand, treating an individual who does not require treatment may also have its consequences, such as learning the "sick role," time lost from work, possible social stigma, costs in staff time and facilities, and so on.

Scheff[11] has presented two Baysian-based equations aimed at facilitating treatment versus nontreatment decisions. Four cost-utility values are required for this equation: the cost of not treating any individual who needs treatment, denoted, $C(O_1)$; the utility of treating an individual who needs treatment, denoted $U(O_1)$; the cost of treating an individual who does not need treatment, denoted $C(O_2)$; and utility (savings) of not treating an individual not requiring it, $U(O_2)$. In addition, two probability estimates are needed. The first is the probability that the individual at hand requires treatment, given the available relevant evidence (such as demographic variables and the presence or absence of symptoms and signs). The second is the probability that the individual at hand does not require treatment, given the same evidence. The first probability value is denoted $P(O_1/E_{q'})$ and the second as $P(O_2/E_{q'})$.

The two equations are used to compute the expected utilities of treatment versus nontreatment decisions. The course of action is determined by the highest utility value. Using the terms defined above, the expected utility of implementing treatment is computed as follows:

$$U_t = P(O_1/E_{q'})U(O_1) - P(O_2/E_{q'})C(O_2)$$

Similarly, the expected utility of nontreatment is computed as:

$$U_n = P(O_2/E_{q'})U(O_2) - P(O_1/E_{q'})C(O_1)$$

The decision rule consists of administering treatment if and only if the value of U_t exceeds that of U_n.

In dealing with this issue, Scheff has included utility values of correct decisions as well as cost values of errors. For example, the value of treating a patient in need of it is seen as involving variables such as the treatment's cure rate, whereas the cost of not treating the individual involves the risk of progressive deterioration in the patient's state (barring spontaneous recovery, and so on). The utility in withholding treatment from one not in need of it implicates savings in such things as medical expenses and working days, whereas the cost of treating a healthy individual includes inconvenience, loss of salary, institutional and professional waste, and potential stigma in some cases. In expected cost-benefit analysis, utility values such as those used here are sometimes omitted in the formal computations; they are considered to be the opposite of costs and hence provide information which is effectively redundant. For example, the utility of treating one actually in need of treatment would also be the avoidance of possible deterioration in the same patient's state. The cost of not treating one in need would involve a similar quantity—the cost associated with the occurrence of deterioration. The possibility of spontaneous recovery can be regarded as a balancing factor. Although it reduces the expected cost in the absence of treatment, at the same time it detracts from the expected value of treatment because an apparent cure in the midst of spontaneous recovery may well be spurious.

The computations of the relevant probability values $P(O_1/E_{q'})$ and $P(O_2/E_{q'})$ were outlined in the first section of the chapter. Derivation of the probability values for specific cases lies with the use of medical, hospital and government records. This phase of the process, involving the insertion of the correct data estimates into the equations, is currently the most vexing problem in clinical cost-utility analysis. These values can be quite institution-specific, and consequently no actuarial tables are readily available. The construction of such tables lies more or less with the ingenuity of the individual clinical staff.

Moreover, what is the criterion for the individual in need of treatment—how does one determine O_1, and, hence, $P(O_1)$? Does the criterion consist of a positive response to treatment; or prevention of personal harm to the individual; or maintenance of the individual's socioeconomic status; or a combination of such factors? The criterion is likely to depend on the aims and values of the clinicians using the formula. It may be easier to view the problem in reverse—that is, establishing a criterion for the absence of the need for treatment, O_2. This approach may consist of an assessment that a patient's status has not significantly changed at the time of discharge, or where it was decided not to treat the individual, of an absence of admission to a treatment facility during some ensuing time interval. Having established the value of $P(O_2)$, the value of $P(O_1)$ is simply $1 - P(O_2)$.

When a criterion has been established, medical records in conjunction with ongoing, actuarial record keeping can be used to estimate the proportion of all referred patients not needing treatment, regardless of additional information associated with signs and symptoms, demographic data, and so on. This estimate of referred patients not needing treatment corresponds to $P(O_2)$. Additional actuarial tables are required to arrive at values for $P(E_{q'}/O_1)$ and for $P(E_{q'}/O_2)$. The term $E_{q'}$ refers to the evidence at hand for the individual referral. As mentioned, it may consist of a combination of several variables (demographic, signs and symptoms, etc). The proportion of patients in each category O_1 and O_2 falling into the cell associated with the combination of data corresponding to $E_{q'}$ can be used for the preceding probability estimates. Establishing the actuarial data for such tables would appear to demand a considerable investment of time and effort for a thorough job to be done. However, the future dividends, in terms of increased rigor of decisional operations, will likely repay the investment many times over.

A second set of data which is less readily available for insertion into the previous formulas is the cost and utility values of treatment versus nontreatment. Again, a degree of subjectivity is necessarily involved in determining what factors are relevant to costs and utilities and how the specific costs are to be determined. The cost values are often made in arbitrary units, despite the desirability of objectively calculated, absolute dollar values. But it is apparent that one cannot objectively apply a dollar value to such factors as savings in pain and discomfort provided through treatment to a suffering individual. In many cases, these values must be judged subjectively. Approaches to estimating necessarily subjective values are briefly discussed in a later example in this chapter.

DECISIONS REGARDING THE EFFICIENCY OF USING SPECIFIC PIECES OF CLINICAL EVIDENCE

Perhaps the most sophisticated developments in cost-effectiveness analysis in clinical work have been made in the area of psychometric assessment. Although these advances have typically been made within the context of formalized testing, the issues they raise apply directly to any piece of clinical evidence used in decision making. The evidence can include a variety of demographic variables such as age, sex, or number of prior hospital admissions. It can also take the form of a composite score reflecting the information from several variables obtained through a statistical combination such as multiple regression or discriminant-function analysis (see Chapter 8). In the example used earlier in the chapter, the clinical evidence was the presence of a certain type of speech impairment. The same example can serve to illustrate some important considerations surrounding the advisability of using a specific piece of evidence.

As mentioned earlier, the posterior probability of the suspected brain damage, given the impairment, was .82, and the posterior probability of no damage was .18. Hence, there is a risk in treating any individual displaying the impediment as though he were brain damaged, since the probability of error in this course of action—the probability that the treated individual is not brain damaged—is .18. We say that *of those displaying the evidence*, .18 are false positives (*FP*s) and the other .82 are valid positives (*VP*s). The probability of the speech impairment, given none of the suspected damage, denoted $P(E_{q'}/O_2)$, was .10. Thus, the *overall probability* of a false positive, $P(FP)$, would be .10 × .60 = .06, since .60 of referrals from the present source were not damaged. The value of .06 is labeled the *false positive rate*. The *valid positive rate* is computed in a similar manner. The probability of displaying the piece of evidence, given the damage $P(E_{q'}/O_1)$ is .70, and the probability of being damaged in the first place is .40. Therefore, the value of $P(VP)$, or the valid positive rate, is .70 × .40 = .28. In general, the false positive rate is computed as $P(FP) = P(E_{q'}/O_2)P(O_2)$ and the valid positive rate by $P(VP) = P(E_{q'}/O_1)P(O_1)$.

In addition to correct decisions and errors associated with the presence of the piece of evidence, it is also possible to make correct decisions and to commit errors when the piece of evidence, $E_{q'}$, does not appear. The absence of $E_{q'}$ will be denoted $\bar{E}_{q'}$. In the earlier example, the probability of no speech impairment, given the presence of the suspected damage $P(\bar{E}_{q'}/O_1)$, was .30 (the complement of $P(E_{q'}/O_1)$, or (1 − .70). The prior probability of damage was .40. Therefore, the overall probability of a damaged individual not displaying the impairment is .30 × .40 = .12. This value is known as the false negative rate, denoted $P(FN)$. In a similar vein, the valid negative rate $P(VN)$ is computed as the probability of no impediment, given no damage $P(\bar{E}_{q'}/O_2)$ times the prior probability of no damage. The figures from the example would be .90 × .60 = .54. These values are listed with their appropriate labels in Table 6-1.

In the present context, the prior probability of O_1 is referred to as the base rate (BR). This value is equal to the first row total of

Table 6-1
Probabilities Associated with the Use of Evidence E_q' Where BR = .40.

	$\bar{E}_q'$	E_q'	
O_1	P(FN) .12	P(VP) .28	BR = .40
O_2	P(VN) .54	P(FP) .06	1 − BR = .60
	1 − SR = .66	SR = .34	1.00

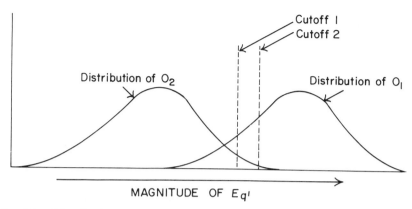

Fig. 6-1. Distribution of O_1 and O_2 along the Axis of Magnitude of $E_{q'}$. The value of $P(E_{q'}/O_1)$ corresponds to the area of distribution O_1 to the right of the selected cutoff, and the value of $P(E_{q'}/O_2)$ corresponds to the area of distribution O_2 to the right of the selected cutoff.

Table 6-1. The base rate depends on the proportion of all referrals who actually possess the criterion state O_1 in the setting where $E_{q'}$ is being used. The proportion of all individuals displaying the evidence of concern, $E_{q'}$, is called the selection ratio (SR). The value for SR depends on the proportion of all referrals displaying $E_{q'}$ regardless of the category, O_1 or O_2, to which they belong.

The value of SR can be adjusted upward or downward, depending on the rigor of the criterion for acknowledging the presence of $E_{q'}$. For example, the SR might be reduced by making $E_{q'}$ refer to a relatively severe form of the speech impairment on some objective scale. The more severe form will occur less frequently among both the damaged and nondamaged subjects. Figure 6-1 illustrates the hypothetical distributions of damaged and nondamaged referrals along an axis of impairment severity. As we move from cutoff 1 to cutoff 2, the selection ratio decreases. The values of BR and $1 - $ BR have remained the same but both $P(E_{q'}/O_1)$ as well as $P(E_{q'}/O_2)$ have decreased.

The SR can be determined by a number of factors, including among others the availability of treatment facilities or the cost of false positive errors versus false negative errors.[1] Typically, the value of SR is determined by the availability of treatment. The SR may vary from a relatively small value in some private clinics to a value of 1 in government-supported institutions accepting "all comers." The SR in

Table 6-1 is .34, indicating that the institution can administer treatment to 34 percent of those referred for the assessment problem under discussion. Accordingly, the cutoff on the horizontal axis would be adjusted to define $E_{q'}$ as the value attained by the upper 34 percent of all referrals.

One of our main concerns in assessing the efficiency of a piece of clinical evidence is its performance in correct decision making, relative to some other piece of evidence, or simply by relying on its base rate of incidence alone. The proportion of correct decisions based on the data of Table 6-2 is $P(VP) + P(VN) = .28 + .54 = .82$. Our expectancy of correct decisions out of 1,000 referrals would be 820. This rate of correct decisions can be compared to other pieces of evidence that were calculated in the same way. It can also be compared to the correct decision rate resulting from random assignment, as depicted in Table 6-2. Suppose a selection ratio of .34 must be maintained due to facility constraints, and that 34 percent of our referrals are randomly selected for the treatment under consideration. In this case $P(VP)$ is obtained as BR × SR or $.40 \times .34 = .14$; and $P(VN)$ is $(1 - BR)(1 - SR)$ or $.60 \times .66 = .40$. Out of 1,000 referrals, the expected number of correct decisions would be 540 or 280 less than with the use of the evidence $E_{q'}$. In this particular example, the rate of correct decisions incorporating the piece of evidence fares relatively well, as compared to reliance on the base rate only.

A more severe test occurs under a different set of conditions, including (a) the possibility of withholding treatment from all referrals, or alternatively administering treatment to all referrals; and (b) a base rate departing significantly from .50. Where all referrals are treated, the SR is equal to 1, and where none are treated, the SR equals 0. Consider a test for schizophrenic vulnerability which is administered to all primary grade school children. We will entertain

Table 6-2
Probabilities Associated with Random Assignment,
Where BR = .40.

	$\bar{E}_q'$	E_q'	
O_1	$P(FN)$ .26	$P(VP)$ .14	BR = .40
O_2	$P(VN)$ .40	$P(FP)$ .20	1 − BR = .60
	1 − SR = .66	SR = .34	

Table 6-3
Probabilities Associated with the Use of Evidence E_q' Where
BR = .025.

	$\bar{E}_q'$	E_q'	
O_1	P(FN) .0075	P(VP) .0175	BR = .025
O_2	P(VN) .8775	P(FP) .0975	1 − BR = .975
	1 − SR = .885	SR = .115	

the possibility of administering prophylactic medication to those achieving a certain score, $E_{q'}$. Let the base rate for schizophrenia be .025. We can now compare the expected correct decision rate, associated with assigning all children to the no-treatment condition (abandoning the proposed program), in relation to using the test to select some children for treatment. (Since using the test implies "selecting some children for treatment," the SR is implicitly different from that corresponding to treating none, where it is 0.) The correct decision rate without the use of the test would be .975 or P(VN). The results from using the test might be similar to those depicted in Table 6-3. The probability of the test score, given the disease $P(E_{q'}/O_1)$, is .70, and the probability of the test score, not given the disease $P(E_{q'}/O_2)$, is .10. The correct decision rate using the test with its resulting SR of .1150 is .8950, less than the value of .9750 associated with abandoning the program and its implicit SR of 0.

Meehl and Rosen[6] were the first to cogently underscore the importance of base-rate considerations in assessing the efficiency of psychological test usage. A value for BR departing substantially from .5, combined with the option of treating all or none of the referrals, are conditions most likely to contraindicate the use of a given psychological test or other piece of evidence for selection purposes.

Deciding whether to use a given piece of evidence implicates both the increase in correct decisions and the balance of costs and benefits accrued through its use, over and against the costs and benefits of using some other evidence or no evidence at all. Furthermore, the cost involved in the mechanics of obtaining the evidence must be considered. This cost may be relatively slight, as in the case of noticing a speech impairment, or it may be much greater, as in the case of obtaining and examining an electroencephalogram. The fol-

lowing formula for calculating the expected utility from using a piece
of evidence has been presented by Wiggins:[13]

$$E(U) = P(VP)U(VP) - P(FP)C(FP)$$
$$+ P(VN)U(VN) - P(FN)C(FN) - C_t$$

where $U(VP)$ and $C(FP)$ are the utility and cost values of valid
and false positives, respectively;
$U(VN)$ and $C(FN)$ are the utility and cost values of valid and
false negatives, respectively;
and C_t is the cost of test administration.

The use of this calculation can be illustrated with the data from
Tables 6-1 and 6-2. Suppose the clinician is interested in comparing
with the expected utility of a test for peripheral neuropathy, (a) the
expected utility of random assignment under the SR as that for the
test, and (b) the assignment of all individuals to the most populous
category obtained from base rate values. According to Tables 6-1 and
6-2, the SR is .34 and the more populous category is that associated
with O_2, representing the absence of peripheral neuropathy in the
present example. The value of $P(O_1)$, which is equal to $1 - $ BR, is
.60. The clinician has obtained an objective estimate of the cost of
testing 1,000 individuals which turns out to be $100,000 He then
obtains values for the remaining terms by scaling the subjective
judgments from several experienced clinicians, using their average
dollar estimates. The utility of a valid positive is scaled at $5,000 and
the cost of a false positive is scaled at $12,000. The utility of a valid
negative is scaled at $7,000 and that of a false negative at $8,000.
Applying the above formula, the expected utility of using the test for
1,000 individuals amounts to:

$(280)(5,000) - (60)(12,000) + (540)(7,000)$
$$- (120)(8,000) - 100,000 = 34,000,000.$$

In comparison, the expected utility of randomly selecting individuals
for treatment is, according to the above values in conjunction with the
data from Table 6-2:

$(140)(5,000) - (200)(12,000) + (400)(7,000)$
$$- (260)(8,000) = -980,000.$$

Finally, the expected utility of assigning all individuals to the most populous category, that of no peripheral neuropathy and therefore no treatment, would be calculated as follows:

$$P(O_2)U(VN) - P(O_1)C(FN)$$

$$= (600)(7,000) - (400)(8,000) = 1,000,000.$$

In this example, the use of the testing procedure is clearly justified.

DECISIONS TO ADOPT OR NOT ADOPT A GIVEN TREATMENT INNOVATION

In regard to the institutional setting, another problem which clinicians are increasingly being asked to help solve is whether or not to change some aspects of an ongoing treatment program or to establish an apparently promising new program. This problem can be rephrased as; Will the cost of instituting a program, which may be substantially better than the present one, exceed the cost of retaining the present one while losing potential benefits of the new one?

In approaching an issue such as this one in the clinical setting, it is usually not sufficient to simply ascertain whether or not the new treatment produces a statistically significant difference on some important outcome variable as compared to the current program. Statistical significance testing provides information as to the probability of the obtained outcome on the selected dependent variable where, in fact, no real effect has occurred (that is, the probability that the difference between the two treatments is attributable to the effects of extraneous, usually random influences on the dependent variable). Typically, our interest is not in whether the obtained difference can reasonably be attributed to just any non-zero effect, but rather, in an obtained difference which is likely to yield a tangible treatment payoff. In other words, there is usually a range of treatment differences which, to all intents and purposes, are too small to be entertained seriously. The critical question is: What is the probability that the true difference between the two treatments lies somewhere in this range of practically trivial differences?—as opposed to the question associated with classical statistical significance testing; What is the probability of the obtained difference, given that the true difference is zero? With respect to the former question, the range of trivial differences is referred to as the Null Range and assessing the probability that the true difference lines in the Null Range is referred to as Null-Range hypothesis testing.[3,4] The present approach deals with this problem from the point of view of probabilities and costs of erroneous courses of action. One error consists in adopting the proposed treatment innovation when it makes no substantial difference to treatment outcome—an effect associated with the Null Range. The other error is to not adopt the program when it does lead to a substantial improvement in treatment outcome.

Consider a situation in which the cost of the first type of error is twice that of the second. Setting the first cost equal to 2, the expect cost of adopting the treatment innovation, given a trivial difference on treatment outcome, is calculated as the probability that the innovation provides only a trivial improvement in outcome multiplied by the cost of the error. This value is equal to the probability of the Null Range times a cost factor of 2, or $P(NR) \times 2$. The expected cost associated with not adopting the new treatment is the probability of a substantial true difference times a cost factor of 1, or $1 - P(NR)$. Let the rule for making a decision be that of adopting whichever course of action avoids the greater expected cost. For the new treatment to be adopted, the probability of a substantial true difference must be at least twice as large as that of the Null Range.

The first step of the procedure is to establish what constitutes a trivial treatment difference followed by estimating the probability that the true difference is indeed trivial. The designation of a trivial difference will usually be somewhat arbitrary. Take, for example, a hypothetical problem where the clinical staff is trying to decide whether or not to institute a treatment for reactive depression. The proposed treatment is based on a "learned helplessness" model of depression[12] and consists of constructing a controlled environment designed to reinstate cognition that the acquisition of reinforcement is under personal control. Because of the outlay in resources and personnel involved in the formal implementation of the treatment program, the clinical staff has decided to carry out a pilot experiment comparing a prototype of the proposed treatment to the treatment currently in use. The dependent variable will be the length of time between hospital admission and a return to gainful employment. A return to work by an average of at least 25 days earlier than under the present treatment is considered necessary for the innovation to have clinically meaningful impact. Other relevant information includes the size of our subject groups and, if available, the standard deviation of the dependent variable. In the present example, the sizes of the experimental and control groups are equal, specifically, 40 members each. Furthermore, suppose that according to available follow-up records on 500 patients from hospital files, the standard deviation of the dependant variable is 30. (Where the population standard deviation of the dependent variable is not available, those parts of the following procedures which incorporate the unit-normal-deviate distribution can instead incorporate the t distribution with appropriate degrees of freedom.)

Calculation of the probability of the Null Range requires computation of the posterior distribution of mean differences. This computation is similar to computing confidence intervals for a mean difference, and accordingly employs the standard deviation of the difference in means. Where group sizes are equal and the variance of the dependent variable is known, the standard deviation of difference in means can easily be obtained as the square root of twice the variance of the dependent variable divided by the group size. In the present example, this value would be $[2(30^2/40)]^{1/2} = 6.71$. In addition, the sample mean difference obtained from the experimental data is required.

The value for $P(NR)$ can be computed as the area of the unit-normal-deviate distribution (the normal curve) falling inside the Null Range. For example, if the obtained mean difference for the present sample were 23, the unit-normal-deviate value corresponding to 25, the boundary of the NR would be $(25 - 23)/6.71 = .30$. The area of the normal curve to the left of the point demarcated by .30 is .6179. In this case, $P(NR)/[1 - P(NR)] = .6179/.3821 = 1.617$ rather than .5, the value required for the adoption of the treatment innovation (given the previous two to one cost ratio in favor of nonadoption).

The required difference in the obtained means can be acertained by obtaining the unit-normal-deviate value corresponding to a $P(NR)$ value of .33. This value is the critical one in the present case because it corresponds to the probability of a nontrivial difference being twice that of a trivial one. Figure 6-2 helps to illustrate how the critical value can be established. Because the posterior distribution in the present instance is assumed to be symmetric about the mean difference obtained in the experiment, the latter value must be such that .67 of the distribution lies above a value of 25 on the abscissa.* As .50

* In the present treatment of posterior distributions, the posterior mean difference is equal to the obtained mean difference. In Baysian terms, we assume a "gentle" or "uniform" prior. However, prior beliefs about the relative probabilities of where the mean difference may lie can be incorporated into the computations. Where these are incorporated, the posterior mean difference will in general be different from the obtained mean difference. Methods for including prior probability values in the computation of the posterior probabilities are outlined by Hays,[4] Phillips,[9] and Mosteller and Tukey.[7]

of the distribution lies to the right of the mean difference, an
additional .17 to the right of 25 is needed. The unit-normal-deviate
value corresponding to an area of .17 is .41. Hence, the obtained
mean difference must be at least .41 standard deviations of the mean
difference to the right of 25. Since .41 standard deviation of the mean
difference is 3, the obtained mean difference must be at least 28,
given the existing decision rules and cost ratio.

The problem up to this point has been the consideration of a
treatment with greater potential effectiveness than an ongoing treatment: In this situation, the cost of erroneously adopting the new
treatment when it makes no substantial difference to outcome is
derived from the outlay of professional time and material resources
required to instigate the program. Using the present example, this
outlay would represent the sizeable sum of underwriting construction
and professional personnel needed to initiate and maintain the controlled environment for the treatment of depression. On the other
hand, the cost of erroneously rejecting a treatment having a substantially greater effect on outcome would largely consist in not having
profited from this effect and its accompanying benefits. In the present
example, this lack of gain would be associated with an appreciably
earlier return to work and its corresponding financial gain, reintegra-
tion into society, combined with the savings in treatment expense
associated with length of hospital stay.

A similar problem involves a contemplated cutback on some

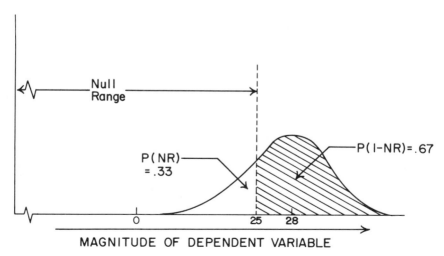

Fig. 6-2.   Posterior distribution corresponding to $P(NR) = .33$.

aspect of treatment or the implementation of a potentially less expensive one. Again, the clinical staff may be quite willing to tolerate a change in treatment effectiveness, specifically a reduction, provided it is not too large—that is, provided it is trivial for all practical purposes. Again, the problem might be approached from a Null Range hypothesis testing viewpoint. Thus, we need the relative cost of opting for the treatment reduction when it has a substantially detrimental effect on outcome, as well as the probability of its effect being substantially detrimental. We also need the cost of maintaining our present more elaborate treatment procedures when the reduction in outcome associated with the contemplated cutback is in the trivial range, along with the probability of the true difference being trivial or in the Null Range. As before, expected costs of the alternative courses of action are computed and we opt for the one which avoids the greater expected cost.

COST AND UTILITY ESTIMATION IN THE CLINICAL SETTING

The estimation of costs and utilities of clinical programs involving treatment, assessment, and follow-up is a difficult task and in most instances cannot be entirely objective. For example, how does one calculate the cost of allowing a psychotic individual to go untreated? Presumably the individual and close associates suffer greatly. Assigning cost values to this factor in objectively determined dollar amounts can be a chimercial task in most instances and subjective judgments in assessing relative costs and benefits are probably inevitable. In comparison, the cost of instituting and maintaining a new program over a designated time period is relatively straightforward. Detailed discussion of a number of issues involved in the objective estimation of program costs and benefits, along with several excellent examples, have been provided by Rothenberg,[10] Levin,[5] and Neenan.[8] The present section deals with some basic formulas for calculating program costs and benefits.

In approaching these estimates, we first need to assess the span of time over which our analysis is to be made. We may wish to estimate over a course of twenty years for a program which is relatively permanent and not easily retractable, or we may wish our analysis to cover only a period of four years for a trial program. In addition, a discount or interest rate must be set for money invested in the program which otherwise would accumulate interest in bonds,

loans, or investments.* This rate is used to adjust expenditures
occurring in the future according to dividends accumulated by the
money unspent in the interim. It is also used to estimate future,
accruing benefits according to their present values. This rate is
usually set somewhere between 5 and 10 percent[5] but will vary
according to current economic trends.

An estimate of the annual utility or benefit value of the program
is needed for each year of the time span in which it is being assessed.
This estimate will probably be somewhat arbitrary, requiring a
systematic set of judgments by several experts. Also needed is the
cost of initiating the program as well as the annual cost of its
maintenance.

The following formula is used to compute the present net utility
of the program:

$$U_{\text{present}} = \sum_{t=0}^{n} \frac{B_t - C_t}{(1 + i)^t}$$

where B_t is the program benefits in year t;
C_t is the program costs in year t;
i is the interest rate;
and n is the duration of the program in years.

Consider an experimental program such as the one for treatment
of reactive depression presented in our earlier example. Suppose our
interest is limited to a four-year period, assuming for the time being
that it is successful in substantially improving treatment effects
according to our present criterion. Let the cost of initiating the
program be a value of five arbitrary cost units of $10,000 (5($10,000))
and the annual cost of maintaining it thereafter, three units. The
benefits accrued after the first year of operation are determined as six
units. Because experience leads to improvement in carrying out
program techniques, the benefits increase by one unit per year. Since
program initiation occurs at the beginning of the first year, the
corresponding value of t is 0. Applying this formula, the present net
utility of the program would be:

* In a sense, this is an unrealistic alternative for money already allocated for
expenditure in a health care institution, as the money is typically invested in alternative
programs or in capital equipment rather than in the private sector. However, it seems
reasonable to assume that the money could be invested in the private sector ab initio
and therefore the present computational approach is still relevant.

$$\frac{0-5}{(1.05)^0} + \frac{6-3}{(1.05)^1} + \frac{7-3}{(1.05)^2} + \frac{8-3}{(1.05)^3} + \frac{9-3}{(1.05)^4} = 9.66$$

Referring again to the illustrative example, this value can be thought of as the increased benefits available from a program that was successful in rehabilitating patients back into their jobs at least 25 days earlier than the ongoing program. Hence, the value may be considered the cost factor associated with an erroneous decision to reject the program. On the other hand, if the program did not yield the desired improvement in rehabilitation, the yearly benefits would be considered lost, with only the costs of the program remaining. The present-value costs are computed as:

$$C_{\text{present}} = \sum_{t=0}^{n} \frac{C_t}{(1+i)^t}$$

$$= \frac{5}{(1.05)^0} + \frac{3}{(1.05)^1} + \frac{3}{(1.05)^2}$$

$$+ \frac{3}{(1.05)^3} + \frac{3}{(1.05)^4} = 15.077$$

This value can be used as an estimate of the cost of instituting the program when, in fact, it makes no substantial difference to treatment outcome. If the present costs were used as estimates in the Null-Range hypothesis testing of the pilot study presented in the preceding section, a course of action to adopt the program would require that the value for $1 - P(\text{NR})$ be at least $15.077/9.66$, or 1.56 that of $P(\text{NR})$.

CONCLUDING COMMENTS

Clinicians are becoming increasingly involved in the evaluation of programs—assessment programs, treatment programs, community programs, educational programs and any other programs that fall into the clinician's purview. Such enterprises are diversely labeled cost analysis, systems analysis, utility analysis, program evaluation, cost-effectiveness analysis and cost-benefit analysis. Each is designed to facilitate decisions regarding the adoption or maintenance of some program. Typically, the Baysian-based assessment of outcome probabilities and cost-utility considerations are similar to those involved in decisions about whether or not to carry out treatment, or which treatment to administer, discussed at the beginning of this chapter.

What is clear is that standard statistical significance testing is seldom the quantitative answer to the types of decisional problems presented in this chapter. Unlike data pertaining to a theoretical hypothesis, where a small but statistically significant effect may be of considerable import, data-based decisions in the clinical setting require a consideration of the magnitude of treatment effects along with potential costs and benefits associated with those effects.

The preceding sections in no way exhaust the issues or technical details involved in decision making in regard to choice of treatment and program adoption. On the other hand, they present the essential concepts of the quantitative methods used to facilitate making these decisions. These essential concepts can supply the raw material for approaching a large proportion of clinical decisions from a quantitative perspective. They can also be used as the groundwork for a more detailed pursuit of this important subject in the discussions cited throughout this chapter.

REFERENCES

1. Alf, E. F., & Dorfman, D. D. The classification of individuals into two criterion groups on the basis of a discontinuous payoff function. *Psychometrika.*, 1967, **32**, 115–123.
2. Anderson, T. W. *An introduction to multivariate statistical analysis.* Toronto: Wiley, 1958, p. 126.
3. Greenwald, A. G. Consequences of prejudice against the null hypothesis. *Psychol. Bull.*, 1975, **82**, 1–20.
4. Hays, W. L. Statistics for Social Scientists (2nd ed.) New York: Holt, Rinehart & Winston, 1973, p. 809.
5. Levin, H. M. Cost-effectiveness analysis in evaluation research. In M. Guttentag & E. L. Struening (Eds.), *Handbook of evaluation research* (Vol. 2). Beverly Hills, Calif.: Sage, 1975, p. 89.
6. Meehl, P. E., & Rosen, A. Antecedent probability and the efficiency of psychometric signs, patterns, or cutting scores. *Psychol. Bull.*, 1955, **37**, 194–216.
7. Mosteller, F., & Tukey, J. W. Data analysis, including statistics. In G. Lindzey & E. Aronson (Eds.), *Handbook of social psychology* (Vol. 2, 2nd ed.) Reading, Massachusetts: Addison-Wesley, 1969, p. 160.
8. Neenan, W. B. Benefit-cost analysis and the evaluation of mental retardation programs. In P. O. Davidson, F. W. Clark, & L. A.

Hamerlynck, (Eds.), *Evaluation of behavioral programs in community, residential and school settings.* Champaign, Ill.: Research Press, 1974, p. 175.

9. Phillips, L. D. *Baysian statistics for social scientists.* New York: Crowell, 1973.

10. Rothenberg, J. Cost-benefit analysis: A methodological exposition. In M. Guttentag & E. L. Struening (Eds.), *Handbook of evaluation research,* (Vol. 2). Beverly Hills, Calif.: Sage, 1975, p. 55.

11. Scheff, T. J. Decision rules, types of error and their consequences in medical diagnosis. *Behav. Sci.,* 1963, **8,** 97–107.

12. Seligman, M. E. Helplessness: *On depression, development and death.* San Francisco: Freeman, 1975.

13. Wiggins, J. S. Personality and prediction: Principles of personality assessment. Reading, Mass.: Addison-Wesley, 1973, p. 258.

7
Clinical Use of the Theory of Signal Detectability

A method of scaling the judgments of patients that has received considerable attention in the clinical setting is the Signal-Detection Theory (SDT). This method has been adapted from the area of psychophysics[8,12] where it was used with the aim of separating two components of verbal reports in psychophysical experiments. The first component was that aspect of the reports influenced directly by the sensory effects of differential stimulation, and the second was the motivational aspect of these reports.

The motivational aspects reflect such factors as the conservatism or liberalism of subjects in acknowledging the presence of a given stimulus designated a signal. The signal stimulus can be a click embedded in white noise or an increase in the intensity of some stimulus property. The true sensory impact of the signal stimulus may be equivalent for both the conservative and liberal subjects; however, the conservative subject may be disinclined to report that the signal stimulus was presented on a given occasion unless the effects of the presentation were quite distinctive and very likely to have been produced by the signal stimulus. Conversely, the liberal subject may report that the signal stimulus was presented even though the evidence from the given presentation might not have been as clear-cut. In this case, both the liberal and conservative subject may render different reports about the same stimulus effects, the conservative subject indicating the occurrence of a nonsignal stimulus and the liberal subject indicating the occurrence of a signal stimulus. The discrepancy in reports can be attributed to a difference in subjective criterion as to what constitutes sufficient evidence to acknowledge that the signal stimulus in fact occurred.

The SDT method can be used to measure motivational aspects of response, such as setting a high criterion for acknowledging the presence of the signal. In addition, a measure of the sensory impact of stimulation uncontaminated by motivational factors, such as those mentioned, could be computed. This measure would be similar for a conservative and a liberal subject having the same sensory experiences. However, their criterion differences would be revealed in the former measure of the nonsensory, motivational component of the reports.

The methodology of SDT emanated from the laboratories of investigators involved in perception and psychophysics.[8,24] Shortly after its wide application in those areas, it was extended to the investigation of certain theoretical issues involved in the study of personality.[17] In turn, students of clinical problems adopted it as an approach to some long-standing issues. Most notable among these issues was the role of actual sensation versus endurance factors in the subjective report of pain.[4]

Application of SDT to problems in these adjunct areas stemmed from the observation that it offered a means of separating sensory versus response-propensity aspects of the overall reaction to emotionally laden stimuli. A number of hypothesized personality dimensions were directed specifically toward anxiety proneness or apprehensiveness about noxious stimulation. Among others, these dimensions included Byrne's[2] repression–sensitization, Goldstein's[10] augmentation-versus-denial, and Speilberger's[23] trait anxiety. Hence, the criterion parameter of SDT represented a strong advocate of its use as an experimental paradigm for investigating these dimensions.

Clinicians and researchers interested in the measurement of pain also gave attention to SDT as a method of approaching lingering issues. In an influential review of pain and its measurement, Beecher[1] had already pointed up the distinction between sensory aspects of pain stimulation and reactivity to the sensation. Investigators were quite sanguine about the potential parallel of these two components to the sensory and criterion parameters of SDT. Pain researchers also have evidently felt that the more recent and elaborate hypotheses of Melzack[14] are compatible with the dualistic sensation–response propensity approach to pain measurement.

Pain was not the only clinical subject approached by SDT methodology. A variety of other clinical issues and problems were subjected to this analysis. Examples of these issues, along with those from the literature on pain, will be presented here, in detail. First in order is an outline of the theoretical model and its assumptions, along with ensuing computational procedures involved in estimating the two parameters.

THEORETICAL CONSIDERATIONS AND COMPUTATIONS OF SDT

The method of SDT is closely related to an older and perhaps better-known approach to the quantification of judgmental data—that of Thurstonian Scaling[25] (Chapters 9 and 10). This approach was designed to handle the differences in judgment about a specific stimulus from one presentation to the next, in the case of a single judge, and from subject to subject as in the case of several judges. The judgmental differences are assumed to result from ambient sources, internal variation of neural activity, random motivational aspects of responding, and so on. The composite effect of these sources is to vary the momentary impact of a stimulus whose physical characteristics are essentially identical from one presentation to the next. The effects of the stimulus presentations vary along an axis of intensity. The mean of these effects is considered the true stimulus magnitude since we assume the values of the effects to be distributed symmetrically. The relative frequencies of the stimulus effects form a Gaussian distribution, meaning that the probability density function of the normal curve (see Figure 7-1) can be used to define the shape of the distribution.

The procedures of SDT represent a case in point of scaling stimulus values using the Thurstonian premises. The method was developed as a refined estimate of the discriminability between a pair of stimuli. Traditionally, one member of the pair was a stimulus which carried a signal to be detected, while the other did not. Examples of such pairs of stimuli included white noise embedding a "click" in conjunction with white noise only, and a flash of light including a letter of the alphabet in conjunction with a flash of light only.

One stimulus in the pair is of lesser intensity than the other in the sense that its effects are distributed toward the lower end of the intensity continuum (see Figure 7-1). In the case of white noise versus white noise embedding a click, the true magnitude of the noise stimulus (N stimulus) can be arbitrarily set to zero; the true magnitude of the noise-plus-signal stimulus (SN stimulus) assumes some

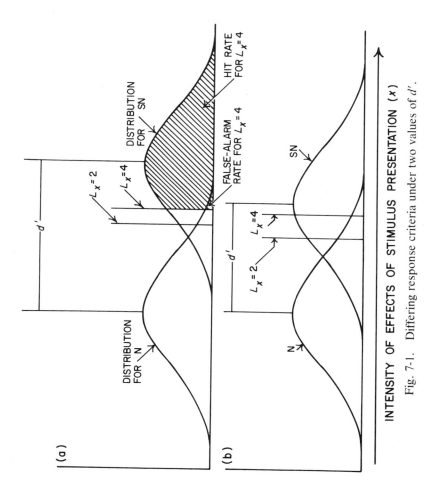

Fig. 7-1. Differing response criteria under two values of d'.

93

non-zero value and is set higher on the continuum. Where the stimuli differ only in the magnitude of their objectively measured physical properties (length, loudness, pressure, noxiousness), the stimulus of less magnitude is considered the N stimulus and that of greater magnitude, the SN stimulus. Figure 7-1 illustrates the hypothetical distributions of two pairs of stimuli, with the difference in physical properties greater for the pair in 7-1(a) than for the pair in 7-1(b).

As can be seen in this figure, some of the effects of each stimulus in the pair are unique in the sense that they are not produced by the opposite stimulus. For the N distribution, these effects correspond to the left-hand portion which does not overlap with the SN distribution; for the SN distribution, they correspond to the right-hand nonoverlapping portion. Given these nonoverlapping effects, the choice of whether the N or the SN stimulus has been presented is a relatively simple matter. However, in the region overlap the choice is more complex. It is assumed that the judge acts as a Baysian decision maker, meaning that he weighs the evidence and makes his decision on the basis of the relative probabilities that N or SN has been presented. Because the stimulus effects can arise from either distribution in the region of overlap, the probability that either S or SN has been presented is never zero. However, depending on which specific effect has emerged, there is a greater probability of it having been produced by one or the other types of stimuli.

At this point, we must return to Baysian-based decision theory as presented in Chapter 6. It was shown that the probability of a specific state of affairs or outcome O_c', given obtained evidence E_q', was the prior probability of that outcome $P(O_c')$, times the probability of the emergent piece of evidence under conditions of that outcome, $P(E_q'/O_c')$. Analogously, the probability of SN, given presentation effect x, is the prior probability of SN, denoted $P(SN)$, times the probability of x given SN, denoted $P(x/SN)$. On the other hand, the probability of the other outcome—in this instance, stimulus N—would be its prior probability $P(N)$ times the probability x, given N, $P(x/N)$. Here, the odds ratio is obtained as:

$$\frac{P(SN/x)}{P(N/x)} = \frac{P(SN)P(x/SN)}{P(N)P(x/N)}$$

It is assumed that the judge has a certain criterion which must be met prior to indicating that the effect has arisen from one or the other types of stimuli. Conventionally, this criterion has been required before a response affirming the presentation of SN is omitted. In the present Baysian framework, this criterion is calculated in terms of the odds ratio above. A more conservative subject will putatively require a higher odds ratio before indicating that SN has been presented, and a more liberal subject will require a smaller odds ratio. Because of the overlap between the two distributions, there is a risk that indicating the presence of SN will be incorrect. The severity of the criterion is a reflection of the amount of risk the subject is willing to take with respect to this error.

Where the prior probability values are equal, they cancel out of the ratio, leaving only the ratio of likelihood functions, or the likelihood ratio $P(x/\text{SN})/P(x/\text{N})$. Even if the prior probability values are unequal, they can usually be regarded as constant from one judge to the next. Therefore, individual differences in criteria should be revealed in individual differences in the likelihood ratio. Furthermore, adjustment of the prior probabilities is usually not available to the judge. Hence, each judge must accomodate his particular criterion through selecting the likelihood ratio required before a positive response (SN present) is emitted. For these reasons, researchers using SDT have focused on likelihood-ratio differences as an index of criterion differences. The likelihood ratio for any stimulus effect x can be estimated as the ratio of the ordinate from the SN distribution to that of the N distribution at point x on the abscissa (see Figure 7-1). The stimulus effect which must be reached for a positive response to be given is that x leading to a value of $P(x/\text{SN})/P(x/\text{N})$ which meets the subject's likelihood-ratio criterion.

Two different criterion values are shown in (a) and (b) of Figure 7-1. First consider the vertical line corresponding to a likelihood ratio of four, denoted $L_x = 4$. This line refers to the value of the stimulus effect x on the abscissa, where the ordinate of the SN distribution is four times that of the N distribution. In turn, this specific value of x represents the cutoff point along the abscissa where the subject starts to indicate that SN has occurred. Any value on the abscissa equal to this value of x or greater will render a likelihood ratio of SN to N of 4 or greater, and hence, will elicit the SN response. A more liberal criterion is exemplified by an L_x value of 2. This criterion requires that the presentation effect be only twice as likely to have been produced by the SN stimulus as compared to the N stimulus. Such differences in criterion may be a function of the personal dispositions of different judges, or may vary as the experimenter encourages different aspects of performance, such as guarding against the designation of a presentation as emerging from the SN stimulus when it has emerged from the N stimulus.

A few of the other features of SDT illustrated in Figure 7-1 should be noted. The main difference between the upper and lower figures is in the separation between the means of the distributions along the abscissa. The upper figure has a higher separation between the two pairs of means than the lower figure. As mentioned previously, the mean of the distribution is considered the true stimulus magnitude or intensity. Hence, the difference between the means of the N and SN distributions, denoted d', reflects the true discriminability between the two stimuli (in this case, the top pair being more easily discriminated than the bottom pair). The value of d' is a measure of the true stimulus properties in terms of differential magnitude of sensory impact.

Moreover, the value of d' is a criterion-free measure of stimulus discriminability, a property which is illustrated in Figure 7-1 in the following way. In both the upper and lower figures, the value of d' remains constant with a change in L_x from 4 to 2. Conversely, the criteria values of L_x corresponding to 4 and 2 can be established despite a shift downward in d' from the upper to the lower figures.

Calculation of L_x and d'

Thus far, we have discussed the meaning of the SDT parameters. We now consider the means by which they are derived. Derivation of these parameter values takes advantage of the fact that the Z scores and the ordinates of the normal distribution correspond to proportions of the area under the curve. Consider the data from an experiment where a large number of N and SN trials (randomly interspersed) were presented to the subject. On each trial, the subject was required to indicate whether the N or SN stimulus was presented. The proportion of N trials where the subject incorrectly indicated that the SN stimulus had been presented would correspond to the area of the N distribution lying to the right of the value of x determined by the subject's criterion (see Figure 7-1). This proportion is known as the false alarm rate (FAR). The proportion of SN trials where the subject correctly responded with "SN present" corresponds to the area of the SN curve to the right of the criterion-determined value of x. This value is known as the hit rate (HR). The values for FAR and HR contain all the information required to estimate the values for d' and L_x. In order to arrive at the value for d', the Z scores corresponding to the FAR value and to the HR value are obtained. The Z scores correspond to the distances between the means of the respective distributions and the criterion-determined value of x. Hence, the Z

value determined by a FAR of less than .5 would correspond to the proportion .5 − (FAR). The Z value determined by a HR value of greater than .5 would correspond to the proportion (HR) − .5 multiplied by (−1). The value of d' is the absolute distance between the means of the two distributions in Z-score units, calculated as the Z score determined by the FAR minus the Z score determined by the HR, or ($Z_{FAR} - Z_{HR}$). The value for L_x is determined as the ratio of the normal-curve ordinate corresponding to Z_{HR} divided by the normal-curve ordinate corresponding to Z_{FAR}.

Consider the following numerical example where the value of FAR is equal to .38 and the value of HR is equal to .68. The Z score corresponding to .38 is the tabled value for the proportion .12, which is .31. The Z score corresponding to a HR of .68 is −.47. Therefore, the value of d' for these results is .31 − (−.47) = .78. The ordinate corresponding to the Z value of .31 is .38 and that corresponding to a Z value of −.47 is .36. Therefore, the value for L_x is essentially 1, indicating that the decision rule for this hypothetical judge is "If the probability of x, given the SN distribution, is greater by any amount than the probability of x, given the N distribution, indicate the presence of SN."

So far only two response categories have been considered, but it is a relatively simple matter to extend these considerations to several response categories. For example, the categories can reflect how sure the subject is that the SN stimulus has been presented, ranging from "very sure that SN was presented" to "very sure that N was presented." In this case the respective categories are successively treated as the SN-present part of the two-category case. The FAR and HR values can be computed for the most extreme category (that is, "very sure that SN was presented") using the proportion of N and SN trials respectively allocated to it. For the less extreme categories, such as "fairly sure that SN was presented," the FAR is taken as the cumulative proportion of N presentations allocated to itself and all more extreme categories. The proportions are cumulative since it is assumed that if the presentation met the criterion for assignment to the more extreme category, it would at least meet the criterion for the less extreme category. For the same reason, the HR value is taken as the cumulative proportion of allocations of SN trials to the less extreme category and all categories above it.

Multi-category response data can provide a more accurate estimate for d'. Because several pairs of HR and FAR values are available, several estimates of d' can be obtained and averaged. In addition, several criterion values can be computed, one for each response category, using the cumulative-proportion HR and FAR values.

Take, for example, two criterion values indicated in Figure 7-1 ($L_x = 2$ and $L_x = 4$). Values such as these could reasonably be expected from three-category response data. The categories may consist of "positive that SN is present," "quite sure that SN is present," and "SN is not present." The criterion $L_x = 4$ corresponds to the first category and the criterion $L_x = 2$ to the second. The portion of the N distribution to the right of the vertical lines demarcating L_x represent the FAR values; the portion of the SN distribution to the right of the lines represent the HR values. In this example, the hypothetical judge's criterion for the first category is twice as strict as his criterion for the second category.

A common multiple-response technique is to employ numerical rating scales. The numbers on the scale designate varying degrees of the continuum of interest such as brightness, heat, pain, or aversiveness. For example, the subject may be required to rate a large number of stimulus presentations with respect to their degree of brightness on a 7-point scale, with 7 indicating "extremely bright" and 1 indicating "dull." Each number of the scale is treated as a response category, with the higher numbers corresponding to more extreme categories. Estimates of both d' and L_x are potentially available at each rating category.

In addition to multiple categories of response, SDT can also accomodate more than two stimuli of differing magnitudes. In this case, the calculations for the two-stimulus situation can be directly extended to each pair of stimuli which are adjacent on the continuum of intensity. The higher of the two is designated as the SN stimulus.

It should be noted that in order to calculate values of d' and L_x using a given category, there must be some overlap between the two distributions within that category. Specifically, the FAR value and the HR values must each be somewhere between zero and one in order to obtain Z scores and ordinate values from the normal distribution table. This requirement sometimes prevents the use of data from certain categories in multiple-category experiments using several pairs of stimuli. It can be especially vexing when applying SDT to clinical data, as will be elaborated in the section on special considerations for SDT in the clinical setting.

The procedures for calculating d' and L_x have tacitly assumed certain properties of the distribution of stimulus effects. As mentioned previously, it is assumed that the distributions follow a Gaussian probability-density function in that they form a normal

curve. It is also assumed that the effects form homogeneous dispersions. The first assumption implies that the ordinates and Z scores
obtained from the normal-curve tabled values are valid; the second is
similar to the assumption of homogeneity of variance associated with
analysis of variance. If these assumptions are met, certain properties
of the obtained response proportions will emerge.

These properties require consideration of a plot of the HR and
FAR data known as the receiver operating characteristic curve, or
ROC curve. For each category the HR is plotted against the corresponding FAR on commercially available normal-normal graph paper
(Figure 7-2). If the distributions assume a Gaussian function, the
resulting scatter plot will be essentially linear. If their dispersions are
homogeneous, the plot will have a slope of 1—that is, the angle
between the horizontal axis and line of best fit for the scatter plot will
be 45 degrees.

Overall, the present treatment of SDT has been designed to
familiarize the reader with the premises on which the computations of
its parameters are based. More technical treatments are available
from several sources including Egan and Clarke,[8] and Swets.[24] A
good source for a basic description of some of the nonparametric
extensions of SDT which bypass the types of assumptions mentioned
here has been provided by Pastore and Scheirer.[16]

It should be mentioned that a number of studies have been
carried out on the validity of the SDT parameters of d' and L_x.[8,16] In
the balance, the data have favored the model. For example, the value
of d' has been shown to be relatively unaffected by manipulations
directed toward the criterion component of the model. On the other
hand, the criterion estimate can be influenced by such manipulations
as a greater pay-off for correct identifications of the signal stimulus,
and negative pay-off for incorrect indications of the presence of the
noise stimulus. Moreover, the results from SDT analysis appear to be
generally refractory to contamination by sequence effects resulting
from a large number of repeated trials.

Significance Test for Differences in d'

A very useful test accompanying the calculation of the SDT
parameters is a significance test for differences in values of d'. This
test is known as the G test and was introduced by Gourevitch and
Galanter.[11] It contains certain similarities to the familiar Z test of
significance. The test statistic is the ratio of the difference in the d'

values divided by the standard deviation of the difference. The ratio is
written as:

$$G = \frac{d'_i - d'_j}{[\hat{V}(d'_i) + \hat{V}(d'_j)]^{1/2}}$$

The numerator corresponds to the difference in the values of d'
between two stimulus pairs designated i and j. The terms $V(d'_i)$ and
$V(d'_j)$ refer to the variance in d' estimated from the distributions
associated with the stimulus pairs i and j respectively. For a given
pair of stimuli, this variance term is obtained as:

$$\hat{V}(d') = \frac{(1 - FAR)(FAR)}{n_N(ORD_{(FAR)})^2} + \frac{(1 - HR)(HR)}{n_{SN}(ORD_{(HR)})^2}$$

where the terms FAR and HR refer to the proportions for these
values that were defined in the preceding section;
n_N is the number of trials for the N stimulus and n_{SN} is the
number of trials for the SN stimulus;
$ORD_{(FAR)}$ is the ordinate of the normal distribution
corresponding to the Z score determined by the FAR value;
and $ORD_{(HR)}$ is the ordinate corresponding to the Z score
determined by the HR value.

The resulting value for G is referred to the normal distribution for
obtaining its probability under the null hypothesis of no real difference. A numerical example is presented in Table 7-1 for two pairs of
stimuli of considerably different d' values.

SPECIAL CONSIDERATIONS WHEN USING SDT IN THE CLINICAL SETTING

As mentioned, SDT was initially used mainly by researchers in
the subdisciplines of perception and psychophysics. Not surprisingly,
there were some difficulties in extrapolating a method designed primarily for problems encountered in those areas to the types of problems
encountered in the clinical setting. Of primary concern in psychophysics was the mapping of relations between subjective experience
and physical attributes of stimulation, along with the possible neurological substrates which might mediate these relationships. The parameter d' was of primary interest because of its properties as a relatively
pure measure of discriminability. On the other hand, L_x was in some

Table 7-1

Numerical Example of Significance Test for the Difference in
Two Values of d' Based on the G Statistic.

	FAR	n_N	HR	n_{SN}	$1 - $ FAR	$1 - $ HR	Z_{FAR}	Z_{HR}	d'_i
Pair i	.20	200	.75	200	.80	.25	.84	$-.68$	1.52
Pair j	.40	150	.55	150	.60	.45	.26	$-.13$	.39

$$\hat{V}(d'_i) = \left[\frac{.80(.20)}{200(.280)^2} + \frac{.25(.75)}{200(.317)^2} \right] = .0195$$

$$\hat{V}(d'_j) = \left[\frac{.60(.40)}{150(.386)^2} + \frac{.45(.55)}{150(.396)^2} \right] = .0212$$

$$G = \frac{1.13}{(.0195 + .0212)^{1/2}} = 5.60$$

Since 5.60 is well beyond the tabled values for Z, the null hypothesis of no real difference is firmly rejected in favor of the tenability of the alternate hypothesis of a real difference.

ways a wastebasket parameter reflecting those components of response that had contaminated estimates of discriminability prior to the development of SDT. For the clinician, however, L_x held potentially important psychometric properties as an index of response propensity—and to reiterate an earlier point, many research hypotheses from the subdisciplines of personality and clinical psychology dealt specifically with that construct.

There were other differences in the clinician's approach to SDT. The psychophysicist was in good part concerned with the change in d' corresponding to a change in the signal to be detected or a change in some property of the initial signal. The clinician was more concerned with the change in d' where the same stimuli were judged under different conditions or by different classes of subjects. For example, he might have been interested in the change in d' between two pain stimuli where the judgments were made after the administration of a placebo[9]; or he might have been interested in d' differences in the same set of stimuli between subjects classified as "high anxious" versus those classified as "low anxious."

With respect to the procedures themselves, a practice commonly employed by psychophysicists was to use many preliminary trials in order to familiarize subjects with the stimuli and the judgment task. These preliminary trials allowed the subject to estimate the type of stimulus effects he would encounter, along with their relationships to the N and SN distributions. In this manner, the subject was expected to better establish his decision rules regarding the probabilities of stimulus effects emanating from either source, and also to gauge the magnitude of effect associated with the critical ratio of probabilities required for a positive response. Because of practical constraints, even limited practice trials were often not feasible in the clinical setting. It had to be assumed, perhaps tenuously, that the subject could set his decision rules using the information he brought to the experiment in conjunction with the stimulus trials as they proceeded. An excellent review of these and similar difficulties encountered when extrapolating SDT to clinical problems, especially in regard to the measurement of pain, has been presented by Rollman.[22]

One of the problems that researchers have had some success in overcoming involves the large number of stimulus presentations required to obtain reliable estimates of d' and L_x. Often the nature of the stimulation prevents this criterion from being met, especially in the case of aversive stimuli. Sometimes characteristics of the subjects prevent large numbers of stimulus presentations, for example, where the data is being obtained from uncooperative or from psychotic patients. A consequence of such limitations in the number of available presentations is an insufficient data basis from which to obtain the proportions corresponding to the FAR and HR values. Where each member of a stimulus pair was presented two or three hundred times, the proportions will essentially be perfectly reliable. Where each member was presented only ten or fifteen times, the reliability is suspect.

A second consequence is the problematical lack of overlap between stimulus pairs with respect to response categories. Where the response categories elicited by the SN stimulus of a pair were never elicited by the N stimulus of the pair, the type of overlap depicted in Figure 7-1 cannot be presupposed. The value for FAR would be zero since none of the N stimulus presentations had met the subject's criterion for inclusion into these categories. On the other hand, it is possible to obtain a response configuration where the FAR is greater than zero, but where 100 percent of the SN presentations are assigned to the category under consideration or to a more severe category. In this case, the value for HR is one. Whenever FAR is zero or HR is one, the required Z and ordinate values for the SDT parameters cannot be calculated because the tabled values for the normal curve do not include these two proportions.

One possible solution is to compute the proportions in the given categories from the response data taken from all subjects in a group. For example, if fifteen N and fifteen SN trials were presented to each of twenty subjects in a group, the FAR for a given category would be the number of presentations of the N stimulus assigned to that and more severe categories out of a possible 300. The HR would be computed in a similar fashion. This procedure usually obviates proportions of zero and one. The group is treated as a single observer because the obtained values of d' and L_x reflect the pooled influence of judgments from the individual members of the group. We can argue that this procedure is similar to the common one of separately computing d' for each member of the group and then using the mean of the individual values to characterize the group as a whole. By computing d' and L_x values at a higher level of data integration—by calculating the proportions only after combining responses from all subjects—the data properties required by the mathematical model are maintained while the data configuration itself is not violated. We can even prove that the proportions based on the total response configuration are algebraically equivalent to the average of the individual proportions taken for the subjects.

However, use of this procedure must be tempered with other considerations. The value of d' was developed as an index of discriminability specific to an individual subject. Its meaning when based on the performance of the group as a whole has not been treated very extensively to date. Furthermore, it can be misleading to use the value of d' based on group-wise proportions as an estimate of what would be obtained if d's were first computed on individual subjects and then averaged. These values are comparable only if the d's for the individual subjects are from the start relatively homogeneous throughout the group.[13]

In order to test for differences in d' between groups, the G test[11] can be applied to the group-wise estimates of FAR and HR values. However, the G test was initially developed to test differences in d' between two pairs of stimuli judged by a single subject. To our knowledge, its mathematical validity when applied to group-wise proportions has not been precisely determined, but some studies have nevertheless used it in this way.[3,15]

Having discussed the problem of overlap at the individual subject level and the use of group-wise proportions, we move to an interpretation of differences in d' under varying experimental conditions. The value of d' was initially taken to reflect discriminability between stimuli, or their sensory separation along an underlying continuum. If a larger d' were associated with one SN stimulus as compared to another, the first SN stimulus would be more discriminable because of its position further to the right on the underlying continuum than the other SN stimulus. This interpretation required that the distribution of N on the continuum be stationary while one regarded either SN stimulus. The assumption was reasonable as long as each SN stimulus was judged in the same experimental context, and the referent N stimulus was the same for each set of judgments.

What happens to two different d' values when the same stimulus pairs have been judged within different experimental contexts or by different classes of subjects? In this case, the assumption of a stationary N distribution, despite a difference in d', may not be as viable.[22] If the N distribution was itself affected by the experimental manipulation, or if it shifted with a different class of subjects, d' changes could no longer be attributed to variation in the SN distribution alone. If both distributions in the pair had shifted downward equally, d' would be unaffected, but no one would regard this as an instance of no experimental effect. Hence, used in this kind of experimental situation, reference to d' alone as an index of treatment effects can lead to erroneous conclusions. Furthermore, if the N distribution alone were affected by the manipulation, the value of d' would reflect the change, but attributing it to a shift in the SN distribution would be clearly misleading.

For example, if the underlying continuum reflected a dimension of aversiveness of some sort, the clinician would typically want the liberty of interpreting a reduction in d' as indicative of a reduction in the aversive properties of the designated SN stimulus. Suppose the stimulus pair consisted of two levels of sound intensity, one of neutral amplitude and the other of a clearly aversive amplitude. Let the treatment of interest be some variety of muscular relaxation. Judgments made under conditions of relaxation may render a smaller d' than those made under normal conditions. The clinician may wish to interpret this result as supporting the hypothesis that a state of relaxation reduces the aversive properties of noxious auditory stimulation. However, since a reduced d' can result from a greater merger of the N and SN distributions, regardless of how the merger takes place, the result may instead indicate that the state of relaxation lent aversive properties to the ordinarily neutral stimulus. In this case, its distribution would shift to the right but the SN distribution would be unaffected. The interpretation of reduced aversive properties of the SN stimulus requires that the N distribution be unaffected by experimental manipulation. When SDT is used in this manner, it should be ascertained that the difference in FAR values under each experimental condition is negligible.

Finally, the utility of SDT in the clinical setting may be enhanced in the following way. It is possible that the separation of the criterion and sensory components of responding may be discouraged because of the elaborate procedures and computations underlying SDT. It is suggested that a number of measures of the underlying dimension addressed by SDT be obtained concomitantly with the SDT estimates themselves. If some of these auxiliary measures are found to correlate highly with either of the SDT parameters, they can be used as more convenient estimates of the parameters. Even where the correlations are only moderate, the more convenient auxiliary measures may be combined to provide an index of the parameters in a multiple-regression approach (see Chapter 8).

EXAMPLES OF THE USE OF SDT FROM CLINICAL LITERATURE

A persistent problem facing clinicians is the measurement of pain experiences. The problem arises because of individual differences in acknowledging pain and in reporting variations in its intensity. These differences stem from a variety of influences, including personality and cultural variables and past learning experiences related to the report of pain.

The methodology of SDT was especially appealing for the problem of pain measurement because of the possibility of separating the response-criterion component of subjective reports from the sensory aspects of the experience. SDT held out the promise of obtaining independent estimates of the stimulus intensity actually experienced and the level of experienced intensity which had to be reached before acknowledging the presence of pain. Impetus was added to this appeal when it was noted that agents directed toward the amelioration of pain could affect either the sensory experience or the criterion-for-acknowledgement component of pain reports.[1] The method of SDT might be used to map the effects of the various agents.

The influential theory of pain perception presented by Melzack[14] pointed up the possibility that central or cognitive factors—such as the informational context in which the pain was experienced—might affect not only the criterion for pain report, but also the transmission of pain stimulation from more peripheral neurological sites. The SDT method could play a role in isolating the net effects of the cognition-transmission interchange on the emergent level of felt pain, registered at the subjective plane, in contrast to the interpretation of the subjectively felt pain.

Because of the numerous repeated observations required for SDT estimates, it was necessary for pain researchers to resort to experimental pain stimulation which could be administered repeatedly and without tissue damage. In a series of ingenious experiments designed to map the effects of several pain modifiers, Clark and his coworkers[5] used the Hardy-Wolff-Goodell Dolorimeter to administer cutaneous, radiant heat pain. This method allowed repeated applications of several levels of heat to the volar surface of the forearm. After each application, the subject was required to indicate the severity of the stimulus on a several-point rating scale. The proportions of responses to the stimulus intensities in each rating category were used to obtain HR and FAR values. Hence, these experiments employed multiple stimulus pairs—the more intense member of each pair serving as the SN stimulus—and multiple response categories. For each pair of adjacent stimulus intensities, a value for FAR was obtained at each rating category. It was calculated as the cumulative proportion of the weaker stimulus applications allocated to that category and to all other more severe categories. The HR was calculated as the cumulative proportion of responses to the more intense stimulus of the pair. Using this method, the value of d' could be calculated for each category having cumulative proportions other than zero or one for both the N and SN stimuli. These d' values were then averaged for a single estimate. The criterion parameter could be computed at each category with proportion values other than zero or one by employing the ordinates of the Z scores for FAR and HR.

Usually only one criterion estimate for each stimulus pair is computed by dichotomizing the rating scale at the most frequently used category, and computing FAR and HR values according to the proportions of N and SN presentations falling in and above this category. The ratio of the ordinate for the HR Z score to the ordinate of the FAR Z score would then be computed as the single criterion estimate.

In the initial experiment using these methods, Clark[4] found that the primary effect of an experimental placebo was to increase the criterion for the report of pain, rather than to reduce the sensation of pain. In this sense, the placebo increased pain endurance but did not reduce pain experience. The similarity of d' values between subjects in the placebo group and those in the control group is reflected in the ROC curves plotted in Figure 7-2. Each quadrant presents the response pattern of each group for a different stimulus pair. In each

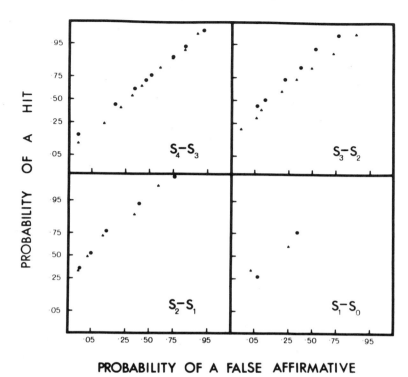

PROBABILITY OF A FALSE AFFIRMATIVE

Fig. 7-2. Receiver-operating characteristic curves under placebo ($\triangle$) and
control ($\bigcirc$) conditions, plotted on normal deviate axes. (From "Sensory
decision theory analysis of the placebo effect on the criterion for pain and
thermal sensitivity (d')" by W. C. Clark, *Journal of Abnormal Psychology*,
1969, *74*, 363–371. Copyright 1969 by the American Psychological Associa-
tion. Reprinted by permission.)

quadrant, the ROC curves for the placebo and control groups are
described by essentially the same straight line. Different d' values
would require that the patterns for each group be parallel, but with
one pattern higher than the other.

Signal detection experiments involving pain stimuli have sometimes employed a criterion estimate other than L_x. According to the
alternative estimate, the stimulus effect x required for a positive
response is determined by some minimum size of effect rather than by
a critical ratio of SN to N probabilities. In some cases this estimate
may more accurately reflect criterion aspects of responding, than L_x.
The criterion estimate, known as the sensory magnitude criterion or

C_x, is obtained as the distance of the given response category from the mean of the N distribution of a pair. It corresponds to the Z score determined by the FAR for that category. However, the validity of this measure when carrying out comparisons between groups requires that differences in d' first be taken into account. Otherwise C_x differences may reflect sensory as well as criterion group differences because, unlike L_x, C_x is not independent of d'. If differences in d' are found, C_x can still be calculated from the N stimulus presentations of each pair beginning at the lower end of the continuum, up to and including the pair in which d' differences occur.

For example, in a case where four stimuli have been used, three pairs of adjacent intensities would be available. If a group difference were found for the middle pair on the continuum, two C_x values could be calculated—one for the N stimulus of the lowest-order pair and one for N stimulus of the middle pair. If d' differences occurred for all stimulus pairs, only one estimate of C_x would be available, that for the lowest intensity N stimulus. Whenever the response criterion for the N stimulus changed, the interpretation of d' would be quite different than if the responses to N were unaffected (see the preceding section).

Using C_x as a criterion estimate, Feather, Chapman, and Fisher[9] replicated Clark's[4] finding for the placebo effect. Employing C_x as well as L_x, Clark and Mehl[6] found that older subjects had a higher criterion than younger subjects for reporting pain. Analysis of d' values indicated reduced sensitivity among older females for a relatively wide range of stimulus pairs. In a study investigating the effects of suggestion on pain reaction, Clark and Goodman[5] found that d' was essentially unaffected whereas the criterion component, estimated as C_x, was significantly affected.

Craig and Coren[7] studied the effects of social modeling on reported pain. They found that the subject's d' was enhanced when judgments of several intensities of electric shock were made in the presence of an experimental cohort who was intolerant of the shock. Further analyses revealed that a more severe criterion was induced by a tolerant cohort, but with no accompanying reduction in pain sensation.

A drawback in the SDT analysis of pain responses is the need to use repeated applications of experimental pain stimuli. The difference between experimental and clinical pain has been known for some time.[1] Among other dissimilarities, there is a marked contrast in the meaning between the two types of pain: Experimental pain is sure to be terminated and the source of pain withdrawn long before tissue damage occurs. Although uncomfortable, the experience can be rationalized as an interesting contribution to science. Obversely, clinical pain is usually inescapable, endogenous in source, and even at times an agent of danger or death.

One way to mend the hiatus between the methodologically eloquent laboratory studies and pain encountered in the clinical setting may be to develop surrogates for the SDT parameter esti-mates. These surrogates would consist of measures that correlated highly with the SDT parameters obtained in the experimental setting, but which happened to be convenient to administer in the clinical setting. These measures might also correlate highly with the criterion and sensory components of clinical pain, although this assumption would be necessarily tentative pending demonstration of its empirical validity.

Another hypothetical approach to clinical pain using SDT is to begin with the derivation of values for d' and response criteria, by directly administering experimental pain to clinical patients. It may then be possible to find reliable relations between the SDT parame-ters of experimental pain, and certain aspects of these patients' response to clinical pain.*

In addition to the investigation of pain-modifying treatments, SDT has been used to assess a number of other variables of clinical relevance. One such assessment was made on the effects of the type of muscular relaxation exercises used in systematic desensitization. Chapman and Feather[3] had subjects rate their experiences of several imagined scenes related to phobias. The scenes had been previously categorized with respect to their anxiety-inducing properties. Pairs of N and SN stimuli were arranged according to their adjacent positions along the anxiety-inducing continuum. The SDT analysis of the cumulative response proportions in the rating categories revealed that the effects of relaxation exercises were to increase sensitivity to the differences between the scenes. It was suggested that the increased discriminability of stimulus properties under conditions of relaxation might contribute to the therapeutic effects of systematic desensitiza-tion and related procedures.

Neufeld employed SDT in a different context.[15] The method was directed to a long-standing issue in the area of cognitive mediation of stress reactions to aversive stimulation. It had previously been shown that the report of subjective stress could be reduced by having

---

* This idea was initially proposed by Georgina Harris of the Psychology Depart-ment, University Hospital, London, Ontario.

subjects interpret a stimulus in certain ways, such as intellectualizing about its aversive properties, or simply not perceiving them. The question of whether the reduced subjective report was attributable to a reduced impact of the stressor properties (reduced felt stress), or to a reduced propensity to acknowledge the presence of essentially unaltered stressor properties, was approached from an SDT perspective. Using the method of ratings, several aversive stimuli were presented to groups differing in their cognitive appraisal of the stimulus content. Analysis of response proportions indicated that the primary effect of these cognitive variables was on the initial stressor impact of the stimuli and not on the propensity to acknowledge stress.

As a final example, we turn to the investigation of perceptual processes among clinical populations, specifically paranoid and nonparanoid schizophrenics. Price and Erickson[18] used SDT in an effort to resolve some of the inconsistent findings regarding size-constancy perception among these subjects. They presented a series of squares which were compared with a standard. Subjects indicated whether the comparison squares were larger or smaller than the standard on a rating scale varying in degree of certainty. Categories indicating greater certainty corresponded to more severe criteria. The value for FAR was determined as the proportion of judgments in which a smaller comparison stimulus was designated as larger than the standard; the value for HR was determined as the proportion of judgments in which a larger comparison stimulus was correctly designated as larger than the standard. The SDT analysis indicated that sensitivity to size differences was lower among the nonparanoid schizophrenics as compared to normals, but that the sensitivity of the paranoids was similar to that of the normal subjects. On the other hand, the judgments of the paranoids reflected an abnormally low criterion for acknowledging a larger comparison stimulus.

A number of incisive experiments on paranoid versus nonparanoid schizophrenic differences in auditory signal detection, including the effects of phenothiazine medication on these differences, have been carried out by Rappaport and his colleagues.[19,20,21] Their results are too extensive to be enumerated here, but the interested reader is referred to the original sources for details of methodological procedures and findings.

REFERENCES

1. Beecher, H. K. The measurement of pain. *Pharmacol. Rev.*, 1957, **9**, 54–209.
2. Byrne, D. The repression-sensitization scale: rationale, reliability and validity. *J. Pers.*, 1961, **29**, 334–349.
3. Chapman, C. R., & Feather, B. W. Sensitivity to phobic imagery: A sensory decision theory analysis. *Behav. Res. Ther.*, 1971, **9**, 161–168.
4. Clark, W. C. Sensory-decision theory analysis of the placebo effect on the criterion for pain and thermal sensitivity (d'). *J. Abnorm. Psychol.*, 1969, **74**, 363–371.
5. Clark, W. C., & Goodman, J. S. Effects of suggestion on d' and C_x for pain detection and pain tolerance. *J. Abnorm. Psychol.*, 1974, **83**, 364–372.
6. Clark, W. C., & Mehl, L. Thermal pain: A sensory decision theory analysis of the effect of age and sex on d', various response criteria, and 50 percent pain threshold. *J. Abnorm. Psychol.*, 1971, **78**, 202–212.
7. Craig, K. D., & Coren, S. Signal detection analyses of social modeling influences on pain expressions. *J. Psychosom. Res.*, 1975, **19**, 105–112.
8. Egan, F. P., & Clarke, F. R. Psychophysics and signal detection. In J. Sidowski (Ed.), *Experimental methods and instrumentation in psychology*. New York: McGraw-Hill, 1966, p. 211.
9. Feather, B. W., Chapman, C. R., & Fisher, S. B. The effect of a placebo on the perception of painful radiant heat stimuli. *Psychosom. Med.*, 1972, **34**, 290–294.
10. Goldstein, M. J. The relationship between coping and avoiding behavior and response to fear-arousing propaganda. *J. Abnorm. Psychol.*, 1959, **58**, 247–252.
11. Gourevitch, V., & Galanter, E. A significance test for one parameter isosensitivity functions. *Psychometrika.*, 1967, **32**, 25–33.
12. Green, D. M., & Swets, J. A. *Signal detection theory and psychophysics*. New York: Wiley, 1966.
13. McNicol, D. *A primer of signal detection theory*. London: George Allen & Unwin, 1972.
14. Melzack, R. *The puzzle of pain*. Harmondsworth, England: Penguin, 1973.
15. Neufeld, R. W. J. Effect of cognitive appraisal of d' and response bias to experimental stress. *J. Pers. Soc. Psychol.*, 1975, **31**, 735–743.
16. Pastore, R. E., & Scheirer, C. J. Signal detection theory: Considerations for general application. *Psychol. Bull.*, 1974, **81**, 945–958.
17. Price, R. H. Signal detection methods in personality and perception. *Psychol. Bull.*, 1966, **66**, 55–62.
18. Price, R. H., & Erickson, C. W. Size constancy in schizophrenia: A reanalysis. *J. Abnorm. Psychol.*, 1966, **71**, 155–160.
19. Rappaport, M., Hopkins, H. K., & Hall, K. Auditory signal detection in

paranoid and nonparanoid schizophrenics. *Arch. Gen. Psychiat.*, 1972, **27**, 747–752.

20. Rappaport, M., Hopkins, H. K., Silverman, J., & Hall, K. Auditory signal detection in schizophrenics. *Psychopharm.*, 1972, **24**, 6–28.
21. Rappaport, M., Silverman, J., Hopkins, H. K., & Hall, K. Phenothiazine effects on auditory signal detection in paranoid and nonparanoid schizophrenics. *Sci.*, 1971, **174**, 723–725.
22. Rollman, G. B. Signal detection theory measurement of pain: A review and critique. *Pain*, 1977, **3**, 187–211.
23. Spielberger, C. D. Anxiety as an emotional state. In C. Spielberger (Ed.), *Anxiety: Current trends in theory and research* (Vol. 1). New York: Academic Press, 1972, p. 3.
24. Swets, J. A. *Signal detection and recognition by human observers.* New York: Wiley, 1964.
25. Torgerson, W. S. *Theory and methods of scaling.* New York: Wiley, 1958.

8

Multiple Regression and Discriminant-Function Analysis

BACKGROUND CONSIDERATIONS

One of the main concerns of clinicians is the prediction of clinical events. Those practicing within the framework of the medical model are concerned about diagnosis, treatment plan, and prognosis. While prognosis is the only part of this threesome that lies in the future, the other two components also represent examples of prediction. The term "predict" means literally to say in advance. But as Rozeboom[18] has pointed out, what is said in advance may only be a more conclusive piece of knowledge, rather than the description of an event to occur at some future point in time. For example, a psychologist may be asked to aid in establishing the diagnosis of a patient who is suspected to be epileptic. The psychologist may elect to use whatever paper-and-pencil or psychomotor tasks are available in the assessment process. In actual fact, the patient either is or is not epileptic at the time of testing. The confirming evidence of the patient's status may be if extensive neurological examination indicates epilepsy. More simply, some criterion of seizure-frequency may be established as the definitive evidence. The problem *presented* to the psychologist is: Does patient X have epilepsy? Obviously, the *real* problem is: What are the chances of patient X being found epileptic upon later neurological examination? Alternatively: Will patient X emit three grand mal seizures within the next week? Many assessment problems presented to clinicians are of this nature—they ask what is apt to

113

happen with respect to the appearance of symptoms "unequivocally" associated with a suspected diagnostic state. They may also ask what are likely to be the results of less equivocal but more expensive assessment procedures. The third component of the medical model, the treatment plan, is also based on prediction. It is selected according to the differential prognoses associated with different treatment procedures.

The medical model is especially well suited to illustrating what is meant by clinical prediction. However, whenever the clinician either implicitly or explicitly hypothesizes about some immediate clinical concern, predictions are in effect being made. Take, for example, the operantly oriented behavior therapist working with an autistic child. He may be attempting to identify a strong reinforcer. Several hypotheses are developed (several types of food are dispensed following certain behaviors) and each hypothesis in turn is tested (the patient is observed for his behavior response to each type of food). In many instances the confirming knowledge is not difficult to obtain, such as in this example. Formal predictive activities are otiose when the predicted criterion is readily available. The practice of using intelligence tests to decide on a child's school status makes little sense when the intelligence test is designed to predict indices of academic success that are readily available in school records. In a similar vein, there seems little point in carrying out extensive psychological assessments on patients if the ultimate criterion for deciding on their status turns out to be the appraisal by the attending psychiatrist. The accuracy of the psychologist's endeavors may increase simply by going down the hall and asking the psychiatrist what his appraisal is.

However, when confirming evidence is not readily available, the clinician will in most instances use the best estimate of what the confirming information will indicate. Best estimation in the clinical setting can be divided into two equally important parts. One consists of the predictor indices available to the clinician. For a given patient, he may have personality test scores, demographic data, the number of previous hospital admissions, and so on. The other part is the method of combining these indices in order to capture all of the available information about what is being predicted. The latter operation is the subject of this chapter.

The specific computations involved in data combination for predictive purposes are for the most part well established. However, the adequacy of prediction rests in good part with the quality of the data being submitted to the computational formulas. If the data used to predict the criterion variable bear no predictive validity, the combinational procedures will simply reflect this paucity of information by indicating a collective nonrelationship to the criterion variable. At the other extreme, if one or two predictor indices relate to the criterion almost perfectly, establishing the best predictive estimate from a moderately large battery of indices is unnecessarily laborious. The methods of data combination presented in this chapter are best used in cases where several predictor indices bear a moderate, though far-from-perfect relationship to the criterion. A major portion of clinical prediction problems are of this type. Thus, *multiple regression* techniques are indicated in cases where the criterion is not routinely available and where the clinician has at his disposal several indices with at least some of these containing moderate predictive validity.

The discussion of optimal data combination has to this point centered around prediction, because this activity is so representative of how the clinician spends a good deal of his time. However, data combination procedures have a variety of other informational uses, including elucidation of the nature of a given criterion variable and elucidation of the number of factors involved in adequately describing differences among diagnostic groups. These other uses will be pointed out in the process of developing the methods of data combination described in this chapter.

GENERAL DESCRIPTION OF MULTIPLE REGRESSION WITH DISCRIMINANT-FUNCTION ANALYSIS AS A CASE IN POINT

Multiple regression is a procedure which assigns weights to a set of predictor variables to produce a composite score that will correlate maximally with the criterion variable of interest. The composite score consists of the weighted sum (or linear combination) of the predictor-variable scores. Any set of weights other than those obtained by the multiple regression procedure will result in a less than maximum correlation between the composite score and the criterion variable. If the predictor variables contain interval information—if they are metric—and the criterion also contains interval information, the procedure is called *multiple regression*. The degree of correspondence between the composite score and the criterion is the multiple correlation coefficient.

If the predictor variables are metric, but the criterion is categorical (representing nominal designations such as schizophrenic versus depressed), the method is referred to as *discriminant-function analy-*

sis. In this analysis the predictor weights again produce the maximum "correlation" between the composite score (designated discriminant score) and the classifying criterion. However, a more conceptually straightforward approach is to view discriminant-function analysis as a method for minimizing the overlap among the classifications of discriminant-score composites. That is, the between-to-within group ratio of discriminant-score variance is maximized.

The assumptions associated with multiple regression center around the distribution of the individual pairs of metrical variables in relation to each other. The assumptions are the usual ones of bivariate correlation, including a linear relationship between each pair of variables; homoscedacity (equal variance of one variable in the pair at each level of the other variable in the pair); and normal distribution of the one variable at each level of the other variable.

The assumptions of discriminant-function analysis are similar to those of multiple regression regarding the relationships among the predictors as they vary with the observations in each classification. In addition, we assume the variance of the predictor variables and their correlations between the respective pairs of predictors to be equal from one classification to the next. This assumption is referred to as homogeneity of variance–covariance and is analagous to the more familiar homogeneity of variance in the usual univariate analyses.* Departure from the respective sets of assumptions can lead to predictor weights which are less than optimal for prediction purposes, and to biased tests of significance on the relationship between the battery of predictors and the criterion.

In multiple regression, the predictor weights will not necessarily be directly proportional to the degree of correlation between the predictors and the criterion. In discriminant-function analysis, the weights will not necessarily be proportional to the size of the between-classification F ratios. These methods take into account the relationships among the predictors themselves in assigning weights. For example, a predictor correlating zero with the criterion can be given a non-zero weight by virtue of its correlation with another predictor correlating appreciably with the criterion. The former predictor is often called a suppressor variable. In using discriminant-function analysis, variables contributing little or nothing

---

* The assumption of variance-covariance homogeneity, along with a test for its validity, is included in most standard research-design texts among the assumptions of the basic "split-plot factorial" or "mixed" design. In this design, subjects receive all levels of one factor (within-subjects factor) but only one level of another factor (between-subjects factor[13]).

to group separation on their own can sometimes enhance the separation when combined with moderately good predictors. Under these conditions they will also be given appreciable weightings. In this sense, the available predictability in the collection of variables is often greater than the sum of the parts.

RATIONALE OF MULTIPLE REGRESSION

Multiple regression can be seen as the assignment of weights to predictor variables according to the amount of unique predictive variance they contain. Consider a problem where the clinician decides to combine a number of variables in order to predict length of stay in a hospital. He wants to arrive at a set of weights such that the scores on his predictors, multiplied by their corresponding weights and then summed, will yield values which give the highest correlation with hospital stay.

For the purpose under discussion, there will be only three predictors such as age, number of previous admissions, and a score on a premorbid-adjustment scale. The criterion to be predicted is the number of months between admission and discharge for a sample of hospitalized patients. The most convenient way of writing the desired equation is in standard-score form: *

$$(8.1) \qquad Z_{ic} = \beta_1 Z_{i1} + \beta_2 Z_{i2} + \cdots + \beta_j Z_{ij} + \cdots + \beta_p Z_{ip}$$

where Z_{ic} is the standard score for the ith subject with respect to the criterion ($i = 1, 2, \ldots, N$);

β_j is the weight for the jth predictor (where in our example, $j = 1, 2, 3$);

and Z_{ij} is the standard score for the ith subject on the jth predictor.

Since prediction will be made for one patient at a time after the weights have been obtained, the ith subscript is not germaine to the equation in its applied form. The subscript is included because of its relevance to the computations involved in arriving at the β_j weights using data available from a sample of N subjects (a normative sample). The data for the present prognostic problem may be avail-

---

* Remember that the standard score of a value x is $\dfrac{x - \bar{x}}{\sigma}$, where $\bar{x}$ is the mean of the distribution of x's and σ is its standard deviation.

able from the records of N former patients. We can show that the closest correspondence between the weighted sums and the criterion scores is obtained when the following requirement is met: The β_js are such that the sum of the squared deviations of the weighted sums from the criterion scores is minimized. This requirement can be written:

$$(8.2) \quad \sum_{i=1}^{N} (Z_{ic} - \beta_1 Z_{i1} - \beta_2 Z_{i2} - \beta_3 Z_{i3} - \cdots - \beta_p Z_{ip})^2 = \text{Min.}$$

As the hypothetical values of a given β_j vary, so does the left-hand function of the preceding equation. The desired value is one where the sum of squared deviations is at a minimum. This value can be conceptualized as the bottom of a quadratic curve function, as shown in Figure 8-1. Note that to the left of the desired β_j, the curve decreases, as illustrated by the left-hand tangent—whereas to the right of the desired value, the curve increases, as illustrated by the right-hand tangent. There is neither an increase nor decrease at the bottom of the curve, where the function is at a minimum, and where the change in the curve with a change in β_j is momentarily zero. Our

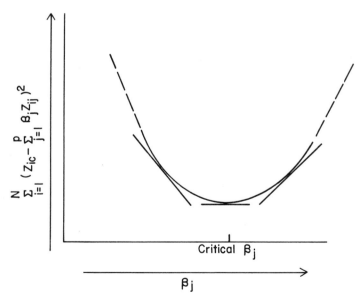

Fig. 8-1. Hypothetical behavior of the sum of square deviations as β_j is varied.

task is to define the change in the function values with a change in β_j, and to solve for β_j, setting the defined change equal to zero. Using differential calculus, by ignoring all β_j for the time being, except a designated β_j such as β_q, the change in the left side of equation (8.2) with a change per unit of β_q is equal to:

$$(8.3) \qquad 2 \sum_{i=1}^{N} \left(\sum_{j=1}^{p} \beta_j Z_{iq} Z_{ij} - Z_{ic} Z_{iq} \right)$$

Setting (8.3) equal to zero and dividing by 2N, we have:

$$\beta_q + \sum_{\substack{j=1 \\ j \neq q}}^{p} \beta_j r_{qj} - r_{qc} = 0 \text{ since } \frac{1}{N} \sum_{i=1}^{N} Z_{iq} Z_{ij} = 1 \text{ when } q = j$$

and $\dfrac{1}{N} \displaystyle\sum_{i=1}^{N} Z_{iq} Z_{ij}$ is the correlation coefficient between

predictor j and predictor $q (r_{qj})$ when $q \neq j$.

The term r_{qc} denotes the correlation between the predictor q and the criterion. Equation (8.4) is more conveniently written in normal-equation form:

$$(8.5) \quad r_{qc} = \beta_q + \beta_1 r_{q1} + \beta_2 r_{q2} + , \ldots \beta_j r_{qj} + , \ldots ,$$
$$+ \beta_p r_{qp} \ (q = 1, 2, \ldots, p; j \neq q).$$

Appropriate values are substituted into equation (8.5) for each of the p predictors and the respective unknowns, β_j, can be solved using the p simultaneous equations.

In matrix format, the β_j are represented by the p-tuple vector **b** in the following equation:

$$(8.6) \qquad\qquad\qquad \mathbf{b} = \mathbf{R}^{-1} \mathbf{v},$$

where $\mathbf{R}^{-1}$ is the $p \times p$ inverse of a matrix with elements

$$r_{jj'} = \frac{1}{N} \sum_{i=1}^{N} Z_{ij} Z_{ij'} \ (j, j' = 1, 2, \ldots, p)$$

and **v** is the p-tuple vector of coordinates, r_{jc}, the correlations of the predictors with the criterion.

Refer to equations (8.5) and (8.6) to ascertain that the relationships among the predictors play an important role in the determination of the composite-score weights.

A significance test of the null hypothesis—that the criterion is unrelated to the battery of predictors—can be made by referring the following value to the F distribution with p and $N - p - 1$ degrees of freedom:

$$F = \frac{(R)^2(N - p - 1)}{[1 - (R)^2](p)}$$

where R is the multiple correlation between the criterion and the predictor variables. The value R can easily be computed as $R = (\mathbf{b'v})^{1/2}$.

Once the predictor weights have been found, they can be applied to new patients. The Z scores for a new patient can be obtained as:

$$Z_j = \frac{(x_j - \bar{x}_j)}{\sigma_j}$$

where Z_j is the Z score for predictor j;
$\bar{x}_j$ is the mean of the normative sample for predictor j;
σ_j is the standard deviation of the normative sample for predictor j;
and x_j is the present patient's raw score for variable j.

These Z_j values, inserted into the predictor equation (8.1), allow the clinician his best estimate of the criterion Z score based on the past behavior of his normative sample. If the predicted absolute number of months of present hospitalization were desired, the obtained composite score Z_c could be multiplied by the criterion's standard deviation and then added to the criterion's mean.

Illustrative Use of Multiple Regression for Prognosis

An early study in which a multiple-regression equation was derived for predicting length of hospitalization was reported by Johnston and McNeal.[9] Their predictors were dichotomous and so their intercorrelations were phi-coefficients. Since the phi-coefficient is algebraically equivalent to Pearson's r, the preceding development of multiple regression is directly relevant to this example.

Six predictors were used:

1. Marital status of single versus not single;
2. MMPI peak score on *Sc* or *Pa* versus peak score on some other scale;
3. Presence versus absence of "psychotic" diagnosis;
4. Anker's chronicity score above or below 19;
5. Meehl-Dalstrom nonapplicable rule;
6. Meeker's chronicity scale above or below 7.

The β_js, in the order of the variables listed, were .298, .075, .185, .057, .051, .212. The highest correlation with the criterion was for marital status ($r = .35$). The correlation of the composite scores with the criterion was .489. Thus, for this sample of data, the best single predictor accounted for .12 of the variance in the criterion and the composite accounted for twice that amount.

SUGGESTIONS FOR THE USE OF MULTIPLE REGRESSION IN THE CLINICAL SETTING

A word is in order about some qualifying points in the application of multiple regression in the applied setting. As mentioned repeatedly throughout this book, the astute use of quantitative methods to clinical advantage is an important facet of "clinical art." The predictor variables must bear at least a moderate degree of collective predictive validity to prevent the prediction equation from operating in an informational vacuum. Both clinical experience and a knowledge of the literature on prediction problems will aid greatly in the selection of good predictor candidates. As will be seen, the utility of the prediction equation is reduced with a haphazard inclusion of "all comers" in the battery of predictors. Research on the application of multiple regression has provided some useful conditions for when the equation is likely to be most fruitful.

One likely situation occurs when a limited number of indices must be combined to make more or less routine predictions. Once the equation has been devised, a clerk can easily arrive at the estimated value of the criterion for a given patient. Sometimes additional information is sought by the clinician who may wish to go beyond the limited set of data regularly obtained for the regression equation. Under these circumstances, the clinician's combination of all the information available to him may be more accurate than the equation's combination of the routinely collected information.[10] Otherwise, the equation will likely be more accurate than the clinician's personal judgment.[6]

A second condition requires that the patients to whom the equation is to be applied be from a population highly similar to the normative sample supplying the data for the equation. Departure from this condition will invalidate the equation to the extent that the intercorrelations among the predictors and criterion depart from those of the initial sample.

A third condition is that there must be a relatively low ratio of the number of variables involved in the equation to the number of subjects supplying the initial data. For the computed β_js to be superior to arbitrarily set, equal weights, the ratio should be somewhere in the neighborhood of $1:25$.[19] The efficiency of the battery of predictors is enhanced somewhat with the inclusion of suppressor variables. Suppressor variables are essentially those correlating appreciably with one or more other predictors in the battery, but correlating marginally at best with the criterion itself. The value of suppressor can be roughly illustrated by considering a battery of two predictors, one a suppressor and the other correlating with the criterion. Variation in the suppressor can be used to identify the variation in the other predictor, which is uncorrelated with variation in the criterion. In a two-predictor example, β_1 and β_2 will be given opposite signs. Suppose that the suppressor does not vary over a subset of patients but that the other predictor does. This variation will be relatively unaffected—a constant will be subtracted from each score but the relative positions of the scores will remain intact. For another subset of subjects where the suppressor covaries highly with the other predictor, the variation in the other predictor will tend to be cancelled out because β_1 and β_2 have opposite signs. In this case, the suppressor removes extraneous variation in the other variable of the predictor equation. When one or more suppressors are present, the predictor-to-sample size ratio increases to $1:15$ in order for the regression equation to surpass equal weightings in efficiency.

Once again, the inclusion of good suppressors in a prediction equation rests in good part with clinical art. For example, the clinician's review of the literature may reveal that marital adjustment is a good prognosticator of length of hospitalization. In the course of his practice, he may notice that the number of different people involved in the patient's sexual experiences bears neither an intuitive nor empirical relationship to length of hospital stay. However, if this variable was highly correlated with marital adjustment, it might be entertained as a potentially valuable suppressor variable.

Several computer packages (for example, the Biomedical Package[7] and the Statistical Package for the Social Sciences[15]) have programs for identifying the best subset of predictors from an original larger set, taking into account the number of subjects in the initial sample. This procedure is known as step-wise regression analysis. The programs compute an F ratio for each of several subsets of predictors. The probability values associated with these F ratios can be taken as an indication of the best subset from among the predictors at hand. However, these probability values are descriptive at best; as with any statistical test, the actual distribution of the statistic under the null hypothesis is affected by data selection from among an a priori larger set of data. The problems are analagous to those encountered when drawing the same inferences from a significant t-test on the most distant means from a set of several means, as one would draw if the tested means were the only ones available in the study. Whenever possible, the predictors should be selected with careful discernment to minimize the likelihood, before the data is analyzed, of including indices unrelated to any of the other predictors or to the criterion. Under these conditions—a priori, judgmentally based selection, as opposed to iterative trial-and-error after the data are in—the significance levels attached to the computed F ratio can be taken with greater confidence.

Emphasizing the a priori selection of predictors is especially important if multiple regression is being used for hypothesis testing rather than for applied prediction alone. For example, the clinician may want to test the hypothesis that depression is significantly related to a history of reinforcement. The criterion may be the patients' scores on the depression scale of the MMPI, and the predictors may include several indices of reinforcement deficit such as one for the patient's social sphere, one for educational-occupational spheres, and one for marital experiences. If the multiple correlation is significant, it will be useful to identify the nature of the relationship by examining the pattern of β_js.*

Other uses of multiple regression in the clinical setting include "bootstrapping."[8] This term refers to the representation of a clinical judge with the regression equation which best predicts his own judgments. In this case, the criterion and the evidence used by the

---

* In practice, the pattern of β_j's, or that of the $\beta_j{}^2$'s, are most often referred to when characterizing the relationship between the predictors and the criterion. However, Cooley and Lohnes[3] have pointed out that a better estimate of this relationship is available from the pattern of correlation coefficients between the predictors and the weighted sums, the latter as represented by the right-hand side of equation (8.1).

judge are quantified and the equation is constructed. Dawes and Corrigan[6] noted that replacing the judge with his regression representation often leads to even better predictions of the criterion than by using the predictions of the judge himself. This seemingly anomalous situation is explained by the regression equation's tendency to throw the systematic components of the human judge into greater relief. On the other hand, erratic and undesirable influences on the human judge, such as personal distractions or emotional states, are downplayed. According to available evidence, such human factors are so disrupting that constant weights across all predictors are more efficient than the personal decisions of the human judge.[6]

Another use of multiple regression involves the translation of test profiles from one test to another. For example, a clinician may be using a certain personality test because it is easier to administer and has greater construct validity than many other personality tests. However, he may be more familiar with a longer-established test such as the MMPI. One can develop (or happily find in the literature) a series of multiple-regression equations, one for each MMPI scale, relating the scales of the administered test to the MMPI. For each equation, the scales of the administered test form the predictor battery. The criteria are the successive scales of the MMPI, in turn. The extant profile can be translated into its best MMPI estimate by the following equation:

$\mathbf{h}' = \mathbf{k}'\mathbf{Q}$
where $\mathbf{h}$ is the 13-tuple vector of MMPI Scale scores
   corresponding to the present profile;
$\mathbf{k}$ is the p-tuple vector of standardized scores on the
   administered test consisting of p scales;
and $\mathbf{Q}$ is a $p \times 13$ matrix with each column consisting of the p
   regression coefficients for the corresponding scale of the
   MMPI.

PATH ANALYSIS

Another use of multiple regression in the clinical setting is the description of relations among a number of events succeeding each other over time. We assume that the events occurring later on in the sequence are determined by the preceding events. For example, it may be of interest to know the relations among several factors relating to a patient's prognosis for discharge at a given time during the course of treatment. The first event in the sequence is the severity of symptomatology at admission; the second event is the drug dosage prescribed after a first consultation with the physician; the third event is symptom severity two weeks after the beginning of medication; and the fourth event is an assessment of the expected duration of continuing in-patient treatment three weeks after the onset of medication. We will assume drug dosage to be determined at least in part by the severity of the initial presenting symptomatology, and post-medication symptomatology in part by the initial level of symptom severity as well as by the dosage of medication administered. It will further be assumed that ensuing proximity to discharge is affected by the three preceding factors. Determining the successive sets of relations for these variables is known as path analysis.[20]

The unique contribution of each preceding variable to any subsequent variable can be obtained by carrying out a multiple regression analysis which treats the subsequent variable as the criterion and the preceding variables as the predictors. The magnitude of the unique contribution from a preceding variable j corresponds to its regression coefficient β_j. One analysis is performed for each succeeding variable. In the preceding example, the required predictor coefficient, β_j, with the second variable serving as the criterion, is simply the correlation coefficient between the first and second variables. The third variable has two predictors, and the fourth variable has three predictors, requiring a multiple-regression analysis in each case.

Figure 8-2 assesses the network of relations among the successive variables by schematically joining the criteria to their predictors with arrows and indicating the corresponding values of β_j. An additional arrow can be included for each criterion to indicate its residual variation. The corresponding coefficient is obtained as $(1 - R^2)^{1/2}$ and is interpreted as the contribution from the combined influence of extraneous sources.

Insofar as it is concerned with defining patterns of succeeding events, path analysis is similar to a previous approach to sequential relations among variables, stochastic-process analysis which was discussed in Chapter 5. However, stochastic-process analysis is used to describe the probabilities of categorical events following other categorical events; path analysis is used to describe the relations among successive events which can be quantified in interval values such as drug dosage or estimated number of days to discharge.

There are several variations in the present approach to path analysis that can be adopted according to the goals of the investigator

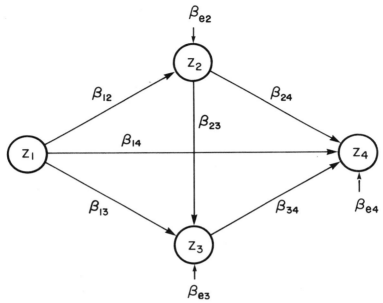

Fig. 8-2.   Schematic representation of path analysis involving four variables.

and the role of the available measures in meeting these goals. A description of the alternatives as relevant to the social sciences was presented by Van de Geer.[21]

An assumption made when using path analysis is that the prior variables in the sequence determine the subsequent variables. As in most cases when the variables are not under the investigator's manipulatory control, this assumption is tenuous. It is possible that some unmeasured variable is responsible for the obtained relationship between a prior and a subsequent variable. Going back to our example, a bias on the part of a physician may be responsible for both drug dosage as well as ensuing proximity to discharge. The relationship between the latter two variables disappears if the effects of physician bias are removed. Kenny[11] presents an excellent discussion of this problem, including a presentation of procedures designed to assess the causal aspect of relations among successive variables.

RATIONALE FOR DISCRIMINANT-FUNCTION ANALYSIS

The rationale for discriminant-function analysis is developed in much the same way as that for multiple regression. The problem can be viewed as that of selecting weights w_j for p variables. The criterion for w_j is that the variance between g categories relative to the variance within g categories is minimized with respect to the weighted sums of the p indices. Visually, the problem can be related to in Figure 8-1 by reflecting (inverting) the curve. We think of the ordinate as indicating the value of the between-to-within category sums of squares of the weighted sums:

(8.7) $$\sum_{j=1}^{p} w_j x_{ijk} (i = 1, 2, \ldots, n_k; k = 1, 2, \ldots, g)$$

The abscissa reflects the values of w_j. In other words, we are seeking w_j such that the following term is maximized:

(8.8)

$$\frac{\sum_{k=1}^{g} n_k \left[\frac{1}{n_k} \left(\sum_{i=1}^{n_k} \sum_{j=1}^{p} w_j x_{ijk} \right) - \frac{1}{N} \left(\sum_{k=1}^{g} \sum_{i=1}^{n} \sum_{j=1}^{p} w_j x_{ijk} \right) \right]^2}{\sum_{k=1}^{g} \sum_{i=1}^{n_k} \left[\sum_{j=1}^{p} w_j x_{ijk} - \frac{1}{n_k} \left(\sum_{i=1}^{n_k} \sum_{j=1}^{p} w_j x_{ijk} \right) \right]^2}$$

where n_k is the sample size for category k;

x_{ijk} is the raw score for subject i in category k on measure j;

and $N = \sum_{k=1}^{g} n_k$ where there are g categories.

Discriminant-function analysis can also be developed in a manner more similar to the development of multiple regression. Since the emphasis here is on the logic behind the computation of the predictor weights, presentation of this alternate rationale may be useful. As mentioned at the outset of the chapter, discriminant-function analysis differs from multiple regression primarily with respect to the nature of the criterion to be predicted. In the present development, the nominal categories are arbitrarily assigned numerical values. For example, in the two-category case the first category can be given a value of $+1$ and the second a value of -1. These values represent dummy designations in that they have no quantitative meaning, but simply facilitate computational procedures.

We assign weights w_j, such that we minimize the sum of the squared deviations of the ensuing weighted sums from the arbitrary category values. This requirement can be represented as follows:

(8.9) $$\sum_{k=1}^{g} \sum_{i=1}^{n_k} (Y_k - w_1 X_{i1k} - w_2 x_{i2k} - \cdots - w_p x_{ipk})^2 = \text{Min}$$

Here, Y_k is the arbitrary value for category k,—that is, $+1$ for one category and -1 for the other, if $g = 2$. The momentary change in the left function with a change in a given w_j, temporarily ignoring all other w_js, can be obtained through partial differentation (an operation of differential calculus) of the function with respect to w_j. Setting this change equal to zero, w_j can be defined in relation to the remaining terms. As with multiple regression, this operation provides the value for the given weight where the function is at a minimum. This procedure can be carried out for each w_j in turn, leading to a similar solution for the respective w_js as was done for the β_js of multiple regression. A more thorough presentation of this type of solution has been given by Kenny and Keeping.[12]

In matrix format, we can show that the desired weights are obtained as the coordinates of the p-tuple latent vector $\mathbf{w}_1$, associated with the largest latent root λ_1. Here $\mathbf{w}_1$ must satisfy the following equation:

(8.10) $(\mathbf{P}^{-1}\mathbf{A} - \lambda_1\mathbf{I})\mathbf{w}_1 = \mathbf{0}$

$\mathbf{P}^{-1}$ is the inverse of the $p \times p$ within-category matrix of deviation-score cross products, with element

$$p_{jj'} = \sum_{k=1}^{g} \sum_{i=1}^{n_k} (x_{ijk} - \bar{x}_{.jk})(x_{ij'k} - \bar{x}_{.j'k})$$

$\mathbf{A}$ is the $p \times p$ between-category deviation score cross-products matrix, with element

$$a_{jj'} = \sum_{k=1}^{g} n_k \left[\frac{1}{n_k} \left(\sum_{i=1}^{n_k} x_{ijk} \right) \right.$$

$$\left. - \frac{1}{N} \left(\sum_{k=1}^{g} \sum_{i=1}^{n_k} x_{ijk} \right) \right] \left[\frac{1}{n_k} \left(\sum_{i=1}^{n_k} x_{ij'k} \right) - \frac{1}{N} \left(\sum_{k=1}^{g} \sum_{i=1}^{n_k} x_{ij'k} \right) \right];$$

$\mathbf{I}$ is the $p \times p$ identity matrix (see Appendix B);
and $\mathbf{0}$ is the p-tuple zero vector,

$$\begin{pmatrix} 0 \\ 0 \\ 0 \\ \vdots \\ 0 \end{pmatrix}$$

The significance of the separation among the categories on the p variables (considered simultaneously) is given by:

$$F = \left(\frac{1-y}{y}\right)\left(\frac{ms + 2\phi}{2r}\right)$$

where $s = \{[p^2(g-1)^2 - 4]/[p^2 + (g-1)^2 - 5]\}^{1/2}$

$m = (N-1) - 1/2(p+g)$

$\phi = -\frac{1}{4}[p(g-1)] + 1/2$

$r = \frac{1}{2}p(g-1)$

$y = (|\mathbf{P}|/|\mathbf{A} + \mathbf{P}|)^{1/s}$

and N, p and g have been defined previously

The significance of the F-ratio is tested by referring to the F table with $2r$ and $ms + 2\phi$ degrees of freedom.

The set of weights corresponding to the largest latent root λ_1 provides the greatest separation among the categories in regard to the weighted sums. These weights would be required if a single composite score was desired for predicting category membership. However, additional sets of weights associated with the remaining latent roots λ_f can also be used individually to separate the groups, but with successively reduced efficiency as the λ_f become smaller. The corresponding sets of weighted sums can each be seen as independent modes of group separation over the predictors. They are independent in the sense that the weighted sums corresponding to each λ_f are uncorrelated with the weighted sums for the other λ_fs. The respective $\mathbf{w}_f$ vectors can be conceptualized as dimensions of variation among the groups (discriminant dimensions). Each dimension is interpreted according to the relative sizes of the coefficients of correlation between the respective p predictors and the weighted sums for the corresponding latent root.[22] For a given set of data there are potentially p or $g - 1$ such dimensions, whichever is smaller.

A test for the statistical significance of group separation on a given discriminant dimension has been outlined by Rao[17] and is available on computer packages such as the Statistical Package for the Social Sciences,[15] as well as programs presented by Veldman[22] and by Cooly and Lohnes.[3] The significance test for the fth dimension of separation uses χ^2 as its referent distribution with degrees of freedom equal to $g + p - 2f$. The value of χ^2 is computed as $\chi^2 = [N - 1/2(g + p)] \log_e (1 + \lambda_f)$.

This test tends to be positively biased—the obtained probability

values are less than the true probability values for the test statistic—
especially with small samples. It is therefore considered an approximate test. Because more than one latent root is available in discriminant-function analysis, Rao's method is often used to test hypotheses
about the minimum number of dimensions required to separate
several categorical groups.

The relative importance of discriminant dimension f, to the
overall multi-dimensional separation among several categorical
groups, is given by:

$$100 \left[\frac{\lambda_f}{\left(\sum_{f=1}^{c} \lambda_f \right)} \right]$$

where c is the smaller of p or $g - 1$

Figure 8-3 indicates a situation where two discriminant dimensions
separate three groups. Clearly, the first dimension contributes more
to group separation than the second.

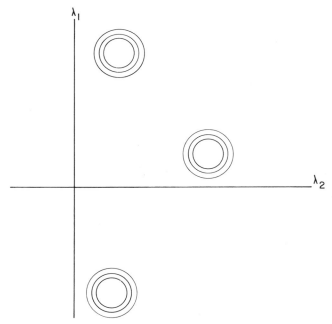

Fig. 8-3.   Group separation on two hypothetical discriminant dimensions.

CLASSIFICATION WITH DISCRIMINANT-FUNCTION ANALYSIS

The following procedures can be applied for classifying purposes, using the results of discriminant-function analysis. The procedure requires that the groups under consideration be about equally populous at the outset. That is, in the absence of any information about the values of the dependent variables used in the analysis, the probability of the case belonging to one group should be equal to the probability of belonging to any of the other groups. This condition is equivalent to equal Baysian priors or the equal base rates discussed in Chapter 6.

Again, a within-category matrix of deviation-score cross products must be computed. This matrix is computed in a similar manner to the previous matrix $\mathbf{P}$; however, the values entered into the computations are the c weighted sums or discriminant scores for each subject, rather than the p original variables. In addition, each element in the matrix is multiplied by $(1/(N - g))$. The required c by c matrix will be designated $\mathbf{D}$. Element $d_{ff'}$ of this matrix is obtained as:

$$d_{ff'} = \frac{1}{N - g}\left(\sum_{k=1}^{g} \sum_{i=1}^{n_k} (d_{ifk} - \bar{d}_{.fk})(d_{if'k} - \bar{d}_{.f'k})\right)$$

where d_{ifk} is the fth discriminant score for subject i in group k, and $\bar{d}_{.fk}$ is the mean of the fth discriminant scores for subjects in group k. The inverse of $\mathbf{D}$ is computed (see Appendix B) and inserted into the following formula:

(8.11) $(\mathbf{d} - \bar{\mathbf{d}}_k)'\mathbf{D}^{-1}(\mathbf{d} - \bar{\mathbf{d}}_k)$

where $\mathbf{d}$ is the c-tuple vector of discriminant scores for the case to be classified;
and $\bar{\mathbf{d}}_k$ is the c-tuple vector of mean discriminant scores for group k.

One such value is computed for each of the g groups and the case is assigned to the group for which the value computed in (8.11) is least.

The formula (8.11) is analagous to a value of Z^2 in the univariate case, where Z is the familiar unit normal deviate value $(X' - \bar{X})\sigma^{-1}$ for a given variable X. The probability of a given score X' in a distribution with mean $\bar{X}$ and standard deviation σ, parallels the probability–density function of the normal distribution (the height of the normal curve) corresponding to Z. As the absolute value of Z

decreases, the probability value increases, and the score is assigned to the group with the highest probability, or the lowest Z^2 value. Where there is only one discriminant score such that $c = 1$, formula (8.11) reduces to the univariate form of Z^2.

As mentioned, this method requires equal base rates of occurrence among the categories involved. Where this assumption is unreasonable, more elaborate methods such as those presented by Cooley and Lohnes[3] and by Anderson[1] should be used.

Suppressor Variables in Discriminant-Function Analysis

An illustration of a variable analogous to a suppressor variable has been presented by Davies.[5] It exemplifies what is meant by additional information being available from a battery of measures when their behavior is considered not only in isolation but also in relation to other variables included in the battery. The separation between two groups with respect to two variables can be expressed as:

$$G^2 = \frac{(C_1 + RC_2)^2}{1 + 2r_{12}R + R^2}$$

where $R = w_1/w_2$, arbitrarily set for the sake of illustration;
C_1 is $2/n_1$ times the univariate F ratio for the first predictor, and C_2 is the corresponding value for the second predictor; and r_{12} is the pooled within-category coefficient of correlation between the first and second predictors.

If C_2 is zero, variable two can still contribute to group separation by virtue of its correlation with variable one. A negative correlation leads to a value of R which is positive, and a positive correlation leads to the opposite sign for R.

USES OF DISCRIMINANT-FUNCTION ANALYSIS IN TESTING CLINICAL HYPOTHESES

Payne and Hewlett[16] presented an intriguing use of discriminant-function analysis following a factor analysis of a matrix of correlations among several measures of thought disorder. They performed a discriminant-function analysis on the factor scores for a group of subjects.* The group categorization was twofold—depressive versus schizophrenic. A new factor of maximum discrimination between the two groups was defined by the following equation:

$$\mathbf{f} = \mathbf{Fw}$$

where $\mathbf{f}$ is the p-tuple vector corresponding to the discriminating factor;

$\mathbf{F}$ is the original p by d factor matrix (where d is the number of obtained factors in the initial factor analysis);

and $\mathbf{w}$ is the d-tuple vector of weights w_j for the d factor scores.

It was found that the values in the vector $\mathbf{f}$ corresponding to tests of intelligence, psychomotor retardation, and concrete thinking were small, relative to the values corresponding to tests of overinclusive thinking. Hence, overinclusive thinking was considered the principle feature distinguishing conceptual deficit between the depressives and the schizophrenics.

Discriminant-function analysis has also been applied to the differentiation between male and female response to a stressor stimulus (slides of homicide victims).[14] Several stress indices were included in the battery of predictor variables, including autonomic arousal, psychomotor disturbance, and subjective disturbance. The sex-difference discriminant function was examined using the correlations between the original measures and the discriminant scores (weighted sums[22]). The resulting configuration indicated that the principle difference in stress response lay in the area of autonomic arousal.

These examples illustrate how discriminant-function analysis can be used to map a multivariate domain with respect to the most salient differences between two designated groups. Since the analysis considers the behavior of each variable individually, and also in terms of its relationship to the other predictors, it provides information in the

---

* A factor is basically a latent vector obtained from a matrix of correlations among variables. It can be viewed as an underlying source of the pattern of intercorrelations. Its interpretation rests on the configuration of the coordinates (loadings) corresponding to the initial variables. A factor score for a given subject can be obtained by summing the scores for that subject on the standardized original variables after multiplying each score by its corresponding factor loading.

configuration of the w_js and the correlations between the original measures and discriminant scores not reflected in the configuration of the p univariate F ratios.

In cases where more than one discriminant function is available, other hypotheses associated with the complexity of separation among clinical categories can be made. Such uses are illustrated in the classic studies by Eysenck and his coworkers demonstrating the independence of neuroticism and psychoticism. The demonstration consisted of first obtaining two (statistically significant) discriminant dimensions. The two sets of weighted sums belonging to neurotic and psychotic patients were shown to depart in different directions from those of normals.

Davidson and Neufeld[4] obtained several measures from three groups of subjects categorized according to whether they were given painful stimulation, nonpainful aversive stimulation (slides of noxious scenes), or nonaversive stimulation. The measures included subjective, physiological, and behavioral indices of disturbance. Upon plotting the weighted sums of the two discriminant dimensions, it was found that the painful and nonpainful stimulation separated subjects from those neutrally stimulated in the same direction on the first dimension, but in different directions on the second dimension. Results were interpreted to indicate both similarities and differences in the effects of the two types of aversive stimulation. The nature of these similarities and differences were inferred from the two sets of p correlations between the weighted sums and p predictors.

Broga[2] compared reactive and process schizophrenics to a group of nonschizophrenics in an effort to test if grounds existed for considering thought disorder qualitatively different between the two schizophrenic groups. Qualitative differences were thought to have occurred if the measures separating the reactive schizophrenics from the control were different from those separating the process schizophrenics from the control. Qualitative differences would also be manifested by two significant discriminant functions. The hypothesis was partially confirmed. Two significant functions were obtained. On the first, both schizophrenic groups behaved similar to each other but different from the nonschizophrenics. On the second, they both departed from the nonschizophrenics but in different directions. The first dimension was labeled a general-deficit dimension and the second a reactive-process dimension. The general-deficit dimension was associated with measures of verbal concreteness, abstraction, and idiosyncratic-autistic thinking. The reactive-process dimension was defined by conceptual overinclusiveness versus concreteness toward physical objects. Reactive schizophrenics were characterized by high values (weighted sums) on the reactive-process dimension and the process schizophrenics were characterized by low values. The values of the nonschizophrenics fell between the schizophrenic groups.

REFERENCES

1. Anderson, T. W. *An introduction to multivariate statistical analysis.* New York: Wiley, 1958.
2. Broga, M. I. Dimensions of thinking among process and reactive schizophrenics. Unpublished master's thesis, University of Western Ontario, 1975.
3. Cooley, W. W., & Lohnes, P. R. *Multivariate data analysis.* New York: Wiley, 1971.
4. Davidson, P. O., & Neufeld, R. W. J. Response to pain and stress: A multivariate analysis. *J. of Psychosom. Res.,* 1974, **18,** 25–32.
5. Davies, M. G. The performance of the linear discriminant function in two variables. *Br. J. Math. Stat. Psychol.,* 1970, **23,** 165–176.
6. Dawes, T. R., & Corrigan, B. Linear models in decision making: A critical review. *Psychol. Bull.,* 1974, **81,** 95–106.
7. Dixon, W. J. (Ed.). *BMD: Biomedical computer programs.* Los Angeles: University of California Press, 1973.
8. Hoffman, P. J. The paramorphic representation of clinical judgment. *Psychol. Bull.,* 1960, **57,** 116–131.
9. Johnston, R., & McNeal, B. F. Combined MMPI and demographic data in predicting length of neuropsychiatric hospital stay. *J. Consult. Psychol.,* 1964, **28,** 64–70.
10. Johnston, R., & McNeal, B. F. Statistical versus clinical prediction: Length of neuropsychiatric hospital stay. *J. Abnorm. Psychol.,* 1967, **72,** 335–340.
11. Kenny, D. A. Cross-lagged panel correlation: A test for spuriousness. *Psychol. Bull.,* 1975, **82,** 887–903.
12. Kenny, J. F., & Keeping, E. S. *Mathematics of statistics* (2nd ed.). New York: Van Nostrand, 1951.
13. Kirk, R. E. *Research design: Procedures for the behavioral sciences.* Belmont, Cal.: Brooks/Cole, 1968.
14. Neufeld, R. W. J., & Davidson, P. O. Sex differences in stress response: A multivariate analysis. *J. Abnorm. Psychol.,* 1974, **83,** 178–185.
15. Nie, N. H., Hull, C. H., Jenkins, J. G., Steinbrenner, F., & Bent, D. H.

(Ed.), *Statistical package for the social sciences.* New York: McGraw-Hill, 1970.

16. Payne, R. W., & Hewlett, J. H. G. Thought disorder in psychotic patients. In H. J. Eysenck (Ed.), *Psychodiagnostics and psychodynamics* (Vol. 2: *Experiments in personality*). Boston: Routledge & Kegan Paul, 1960.

17. Rao, C. R. *Advanced statistical methods in biometric research.* New York: Wiley, 1962, p. 364.

18. Rozeboom, W. W. *Foundations of the theory of prediction.* Homewood, Ill.: Dorsey, 1966.

19. Schmidt, F. L. The relative efficiency of regression and simple unit predictor weights in applied differential psychology. *Educ. Psychol. Meas.,* 1971, **31,** 699–714.

20. Tukey, J. W. Causation, regression, and path analysis. In O. Kepmthorne (Ed.), *Statistical mathematics.* New York: Stechert-Hafner, 1964.

21. Van de Geer, J. P. Introduction to multivariate statistics for the social sciences. San Francisco: Freeman, 1971, p. 112.

22. Veldman, D. J. Fortran programming for the behavioral sciences. New York: Holt, Rinehart & Winston, 1967, p. 273.

9
Canonical Correlation

GENERAL DESCRIPTION

Canonical correlation is an extension of multiple regression (discussed in Chapter 8). The aim of multiple regression is to maximize the correlation between the weighted sum of a set of p predictor variables and a *single* criterion variable; the aim of canonical correlation is to maximize the correlation between the weighted sum of a set of p predictor variables and the weighted sum of a *set* of z criterion variables. The correlation coefficient is computed across the N subjects in the sample. The schema presented in Table 9-1 illustrates the layout of the analysis. Any set of weights $a_q(q = 1, 2, \ldots, p)$ for the first set, and $b_c(c = 1, 2, \ldots, z)$ for the second set, other than those provided by the canonical correlation, will produce a correlation between the weighted sums $\hat{X}$ and $\hat{Y}$, which is less than the maximum available, given the obtained data.

For readers familiar with *factor analysis*[11] (see also p. 133, footnote), canonical correlation can be viewed from an alternate perspective. Kettenring[15] presented a formal demonstration and proof for this approach. Suppose that the variables within each set are intercorrelated among themselves. In addition, each resulting correlation matrix was submitted to a separate factor analysis. This approach presents canonical correlation as an index of the degree of latent overlap between the emergent unrotated factors from the two separate sets. If the p sets of subjects' factor scores for the p (principle)

Table 9-1

Schematic Layout of Data Synthesis in Canonical
Correlation.

$$
\begin{array}{llllll}
a_1x_{11} & + & a_2x_{12} & + \cdots + & a_qx_{1q} & + \cdots + & a_px_{1p} & = \hat{X}_1; \\
a_1x_{21} & + & a_2x_{22} & + \cdots + & a_qx_{2q} & + \cdots + & a_px_{2p} & = \hat{X}_2; \\
\vdots & & \vdots & & g0 & & \vdots & & \vdots \\
a_1x_{i1} & + & a_2x_{i2} & + \cdots + & a_qx_{iq} & + \cdots + & a_px_{ip} & = \hat{X}_i; \\
\vdots & & \vdots & & \vdots & & \vdots & & \vdots \\
a_1x_{N1} & + & a_2x_{N2} & + \cdots + & a_qx_{Nq} & + \cdots + & a_px_{Np} & = \hat{X}_N; \\
\hat{Y}_1 & = & b_1y_{11} & + & b_2y_{12} & + \cdots + & b_cx_{1c} & + \cdots + & b_zx_{1z} \\
\hat{Y}_2 & = & b_1y_{21} & + & b_2y_{22} & + \cdots + & b_cy_{2c} & + \cdots + & b_zy_{2z} \\
\vdots & & \vdots & & \vdots & & \vdots & & \vdots \\
\hat{Y}_i & = & b_1y_{i1} & + & b_2y_{i2} & + \cdots + & b_cy_{ic} & + \cdots + & b_zy_{iz} \\
\vdots & & \vdots & & \vdots & & \vdots & & \vdots \\
\hat{Y}_N & = & b_1y_{N1} & + & b_2y_{N2} & + \cdots + & b_cy_{Nc} & + \cdots + & b_zy_{Nz}
\end{array}
$$

factors from the first factor solution* and the z sets of factor scores
for the z factors from the second factor solution are intercorrelated
among each other, the $(p + z) \times (p + z)$ matrix of intercorrelations
can in turn be factor analyzed. The first latent root (see Appendix B)
of this analysis, minus 1, is equivalent to the canonical correlation
between the two sets of variables. In this sense, canonical correlation
is an index of the resemblance between the independent components
of covariation (orthogonal factors) from the two sets of variables.

Canonical correlation is especially well suited to clinical problems in which it is difficult to specify a single variable that captures
the criterion to be predicted. Often the clinician is interested in
predicting a construct such as post-discharge adjustment among
patients treated in an institution. This example illustrates a diffuse
criterion encompassing a number of variables from marital, social,
and occupational domains. The canonical correlation analysis can be
used to condense a great deal of information inherent in the $p + z$
variables by describing the nature of the strongest relationship
between the two sets.

Canonical correlation analysis is often used to test hypotheses
regarding the relationship between two multivariate domains. For

* The correlation matrices are assumed to be Grammian (cf. 11) inasmuch as there
are no negative latent roots and the number of latent vectors which can be computed
from a given matrix is equal to the order of the matrix (e.g. p latent vectors are
available from a $p \times p$ matrix of intercorrelations).

example, a clinican suspects that a number of dispositional variables are relevant to certain aspects of treatment outcome. The treatment is some form of assertive training; the dispositional variables are scores on the scales of a personality inventory or symptom checklist; and the outcome variables are several indices of stress during interpersonal activities. The analysis would throw into relief the latent relationships between the dispositional and the outcome variables. As illustrated here, canonical correlation is the method of choice for a number of clinical problems. Treatment considerations are usually multifaceted and must be represented by a set of variables, while the treated entity also is often a syndrome or aggregate of symptoms—a second set of variables.

The potential value of canonical correlation for testing more theoretical hypotheses has not been greatly exploited. It can be considerably useful for identifying the degree and nature of a relationship between a causal domain and an effect domain. Causal inferences are, of course, limited by the amount of manipulatory control available to the researcher. However, without some indication of a systematic relationship between the suspected multivariate causal agent and the designated effects, it is unlikely that a causal link will ultimately be established. Canonical correlation can be valuable in assessing the relationship between two multifaceted spheres. For example, we can hypothesize that a history of noncontingent reward and punishment leading to a state of learned helplessness[20] is related to symptoms of clinical depression. The researcher may have at his disposal several measures of noncontingent reward and punishment from the marital, social, and occupational histories of a number of patients. In addition, scores on several dimensions of depression[19,23] are available for these patients. Canonical correlation can be used to test for a relationship between the domains of learned helplessness and clinical depression as indexed by the two sets of available measures.

In addition to the maximum correlation between two sets of variables (the first canonical correlation), additional correlations can be computed (second, third, etc. canonical correlations). The weighted sums of the two sets of variables for all ensuing canonical correlations are independent of (uncorrelated with) the sums involved in the preceding canonical correlations. The values of the successive canonical correlations also become progressively smaller.

After the canonical correlations have been computed, the correlation coefficients between the constituent variables in each set and the respective weighted sums for that set can be obtained. The configuration of these correlations are of considerable advantage in interpreting the nature of the weighted sums.[4]

CANONICAL CORRELATION IN MATRIX NOTATION

The most succinct method of presenting the computations involved in canonical correlation is by using its constituent matrix operations. Rigorous derivations of the operations are quite complex and can be found in a presentation by Anderson.[1] Computer programs for these operations are available in packages such as the Biomedical Computer Programs[5] and the Statistical Package for the Social Sciences[17] It is important that the user have an understanding of the types of operations involved in the analyses carried out on the raw data submitted to these programs.

Four matrices of intercorrelations are required, including a $p \times p$ matrix, $\mathbf{R}_{pp}$; a $z \times z$ matrix, $\mathbf{R}_{zz}$; a $p \times z$ matrix, $\mathbf{R}_{pz}$; and a $z \times p$ matrix, $\mathbf{R}_{zp}$. These matrices can be defined most directly in terms of their constituent elements (see Appendix B).

Element $r_{qq'}$, $(q, q' = 1, 2, \ldots, p)$ of matrix $\mathbf{R}_{pp}$ is the correlation between variable q and variable q' of the first set;
element $r_{cc'}(c, c' = 1, 2, \ldots, z)$ of matrix $\mathbf{R}_{zz}$ is the correlation between variable c and c' of the second set;
element $r_{qc}(q = 1, 2, \ldots, p; c = 1, 2, \ldots, z)$ of matrix $\mathbf{R}_{pz}$ is the correlation between variable q of the first set and variable c of the second set;
and element r_{cq} is the correlation between variable c of the second set and variable q of the first set.

The successive canonical correlations between the two sets of variables are obtained as the square roots of the latent roots, λ_f, of the $z \times z$ matrix $\mathbf{R}_{zz}^{-1}\mathbf{R}_{zp}\mathbf{R}_{pp}^{-1}\mathbf{R}_{pz}$ ($f = 1, 2, \ldots, p$, where $p < z$; and $f = 1, 2, \ldots, z$, where $z < p$). The coefficients $b_c(c = 1, 2, \ldots, z)$ applied to the standardized scores* of the second set of variables in obtaining the fth canonical correlation $(\lambda_f)^{1/2}$, consist of the elements of the z-tuple latent vector, $\mathbf{b}_f$ of the latent root λ_f (see Appendix B for the

---

* The standardized score for subject i on variable q is equal to $\dfrac{X_{iq} - \bar{X}_{\cdot q}}{\sigma_q}$
where X_{iq} is the raw score of subject i on variable q;
$\bar{X}_{\cdot q}$ is the mean for the N subjects on variable q;
and σ_q is the standard deviation for the N subjects on variable q.

computational procedures). The weight for variable q is the qth coordinate of $\mathbf{b}_f$. The corresponding weights applied to the standardized scores of the first set of variables consist of the elements of the p-tuple vector:

$$\mathbf{a}_f \text{ formed as } \mathbf{R}_{pp}^{-1}\mathbf{R}_{pz}\mathbf{b}_f/(\lambda_f)^{1/2}$$

A significance test is available for the null hypothesis that the overlap between the two sets of variables is attributable to random rather than systematic sources of covariation.[2] The test first requires the computation of this index:

$$\Lambda = (1 - \lambda_1)(1 - \lambda_2)(1 - \lambda_3)(\ldots)(1 - \lambda_p)$$
where $p < z$.

The following value is then referred to the χ^2 distribution with degrees of freedom equal to pz:

(9.1) $-1[n - .5(p + z + 1] \text{Log}_e \Lambda$
                          where $n = N - 1$.

If this test is significant at some designated level (e.g. $\propto = .05$), it is tenable to conclude that there is a systematic relationship between the collection of variables in the first set and those in the second set. However, the investigator may also be interested in whether overlap other than that associated with the first canonical correlation also represents systematic covariation between the two sets. A modification of the previous test can be used to assess the residual between-set covariation which is independent of all preceding canonical correlations. The index Λ required to test for such residual, after d canonical correlations have been computed ($d = 1, 2, 3, \ldots, p - 1$) is obtained using the formula:

$$\Lambda = (1 - \lambda_f)(1 - \lambda_{f+1})(1 - \lambda_{f+2})(\ldots)(1 - \lambda_p),$$
where $f = d + 1$.

The value referred to the χ^2 distribution is computed in the same way as that described in equation (9.1), inserting the appropriate value of Λ, and using $(p - d)(z - d)$ degrees of freedom.

Users of these significance tests should take care to interpret their meaning correctly. The test described in equation (9.1) is used to estimate systematic covariation residing in the total of the p canonical correlations considered cumulatively. Similarly, the test for residual systematic covariation, based in the remaining relationships after the first d canonical correlations have been removed, treats the remaining $p - d$ canonical correlations collectively. In practice the interpretation of the significance of the fth canonical correlation is often based on a questionable deduction: If a test of the residual relationship between the two sets of variables is significant with the covariation contributed by λ_f included, but is not significant upon its exclusion, then λ_f has been responsible for the significant relationship. Instead, the test should be utilized as an omnibus statistic treating the residual configurations of overlap simultaneously, in the same way that the familiar F test simultaneously treats a collection of differences among means.

Another caution should be mentioned regarding the amount of confidence to be placed in the probability values associated with the respective significance tests. Like those χ^2 tests used in discriminant-function analysis (discussed in Chapter 8), the present tests give *approximate* probability values only, and consequently should not be taken literally. Indeed, Harris[12] recently argued that these tests are seriously biased in a positive direction—that is, the probability levels associated with the χ^2 values are distorted downward such that significance is overestimated. It is suggested here that the significance tests not be ignored, but that considerable caution be exercised in their interpretation. They can be used as rough guides in deciding how many canonical correlations to consider in detail, rather than as accurate indices of the probability of the null hypothesis of no residual relationship.

In order to describe the composition of the weighted sums produced by the canonical correlations, we obtain vectors of correlations between the constituent variables in each set and the weighted sums for the set. The p-tuple vectors for the first set are denoted $\mathbf{v}_f$ and the z-tuple vectors for the second set are denoted $\mathbf{w}_f (f = 1, 2, \ldots, p; p < z)$. The elements of these vectors can be computed directly using the usual Pearson formula. For example, the element v_q of vector $\mathbf{v}_1$ can be obtained as:

$$\frac{1}{N} \sum_{i=1}^{N} \frac{(x_{iq} - \bar{x}_{\cdot q})}{\sigma_x} \frac{\left[\hat{X}_i - \left(\frac{1}{N} \sum_{i=1}^{N} \hat{X}_i \right) \right]}{\sigma_{\hat{X}}}$$

Or, they can be computed as:

$$\mathbf{v}_f = \mathbf{R}_{pp}\mathbf{a}_f;$$
$$\mathbf{w}_f = \mathbf{R}_{zz}\mathbf{b}_f.$$

A useful statistic for elucidating the nature of the overlap between two sets of variables is the index of redundancy presented by Stewart and Love.[22] The index can be used to estimate the degree of repetitiveness of the variance involved in one set of variables, given the variance from the other set. Cooley and Lohnes[4] and more recently Gleason,[7] have endorsed this index as a useful adjunct to the usual canonical correlation procedures.

One such index can be computed for each canonical correlation retained for detailed consideration. For the first set of variables, the redundancy index corresponding to the fth canonical correlation is given as:

$$R_{\hat{X}f} = (\mathbf{v}'_f \mathbf{v}_f/p)\lambda_f$$

The corresponding value for the second set of variables is given as:

$$R_{\hat{Y}f} = (\mathbf{w}'_f \mathbf{w}_f/z)\lambda_f$$

An estimate of overall redundancy for the first set, given the information from the second set as lodged in the retained canonical correlations, is obtained by summing the $R_{\hat{X}f}$ coefficients; a similar overall index is obtained for the second set by summing the respective $R_{\hat{Y}f}$ coefficients.

As mentioned, this index is useful for estimating what proportion of variation in one set is related to variation in a second set. For example, if indices of reinforcement deficit are being related to dimensions of clinical depression, the investigator may want to know how much of his depression domain (set two) is related to the domain of learned helplessness (set one). Although the usual canonical correlation analysis may indicate high covariation between the weighted sums of the two sets, only a small proportion of the total variation in the second set may be related to that in the first.

The index of redundancy is somewhat analogous to the familiar r^2, where r is the Pearson coefficient of correlation between two variables. The value for r^2 indicates the proportion of variance for one of the variables that is predictable from variance in the other. The square of the canonical correlation between two sets of variables

indicates the proportion of variance in the weighted sums for one of
the sets, which is predictable from the weighted sums for the other
set. However, there may be considerable variation among the constituent variables which is not expressed in the respective weighted
sums. The redundancy analysis allows the investigator to estimate
that proportion of variance in one set of variables accounted for by
the alternate set, taking into account the fact that some variables may
contribute minimally to the weighted sums.

Where there are only two variables, r^2 applies interchangeably to
both. However, the present redundancy measure is not identical for
the two sets of variables. It is possible for one set to encapsulate most
of the variation in the other set, but it may also have a considerable
amount of additional variation. For example, a battery of tests
measuring a large number of intellectual abilities may incorporate all
the information about between-subject differences provided by a pair
of tests for verbal ability. However, the more inclusive test battery
also contains information relevant to numerical ability, spatial ability,
and social skills. In this instance, the twofold, verbal ability battery is
highly redundant to the more comprehensive battery.

A final note of caution is in order. As with most multivariate
procedures of this nature (such as discriminant-function analysis and
multiple regression), investigators should adopt a healthy skepticism
about the specific weighting coefficients in the vectors a_f and b_f. The
coefficients are affected not only by variation in their corresponding
variables, but also by the behavior of all other variables in the set.
Hence, the coefficients may be quite unreliable, especially with small
samples and with a relatively small canonical correlation coefficient,
even if the latter is statistically significant. Before applying the
weights to prediction problems or building theoretical formulations
around them, their reliability should be ascertained using additional
subject samples. We do not mean that results from initial investiga-
tions should be kept private, but that inferences from a "fine-
grained" analysis of the coefficients should be deferred pending
replication.

ILLUSTRATIVE USE OF CANONICAL CORRELATION IN THE CLINICAL SETTING

One of the well-known primary symptoms of patients classified
as schizophrenic is cognitive deficit or "thought disorder." A number
of diagnostic variables (such as paranoid–nonparanoid, process-reac-

tive status, etc.) and demographic variables (age, education) further characterizes these patients. A description of the relationships between the thought disorder and diagnostic-demographic domains in quantitative terms was considered by Neufeld and Broga[16] to be of potential practical and theoretical importance. In this study, canonical correlation analysis was applied to selected variables from each domain using a sample of twenty-eight schizophrenic inpatients.

The variables for each set are listed in Table 9-2. The analysis yielded a first canonical correlation of .98, and second of .96. Overlap between the two sets was significant before removal of the first canonical correlation ($\chi^2 = 186$, $df = 117$, $p < .0009$) as was the residual overlap after its removal ($\chi^2 = 136$, $df = 96$, $p < .004$). Thus, the first two sets of weighted sums were retained for interpretation.

To facilitate description of the weighted sums, their correlations with the original variables were computed. These values are presented in Table 9-2. Because the data is presented primarily for the purpose of illustration, only the variables with the higher correlations will be discussed. The weighted sums for the first set corresponding to the first canonical correlation were described primarily by drug dosage (calculated as chlorpromazine equivalence in milligrams), age, and total cumulative hospitalization. They were moderately related to the paranoid–nonparanoid index$_1$ which was taken from the Symptom-Sign Inventory[6] (higher scores indicated paranoia). The paranoid–nonparanoid index correlated positively with the weighted sums and the correlations of the remaining three variables were negative. Based on this configuration, the weighted sums were interpreted as reflecting a nonchronic paranoid dimension.

The corresponding weighted sums for set two were described by:

1. A negative correlation with a measure of concreteness, and positive correlations with measures of abstraction and overinclusiveness, with all three measures taken from an object-sorting test.[13]
2. A positive correlation with a measure of autistic responding and a negative correlation with a measure of concreteness, both taken from a proverb-interpretation test.[21]
3. Negative correlations with "M" and "K," measures of latency in carrying out two different aspects of processing information in single sentences, according to a model developed by Carpenter and Just[3].

Based on the sizes and directions of these correlations, the weighted sums reflected a dimension of rich but unusual responding.

Table 9-2

Correlations between Constituent Variables and
Weighted Sums.

Set 1		
Canonical Correlation	*1*	*2*
Age	−.42	−.03
Verbal I.Q. (WAIS-Clark)[18]	.26	.40
Education (years)	.38	.41
Occupational Status of Patient[14]	−.12	−.16
Occupational Status of Father[14]	−.13	−.19
Social Position Index[14]	−.27	−.00
Hospitalization (cumulative)	−.41	−.17
Proportion of Time Spent in Hospital since Age 13	−.16	−.14
Drug Dosage	−.61	−.54
Normal–Personal Illness Index[6]	.11	−.34
Neuroticism–Psychoticism Index[6]	.07	−.36
Paranoid–Nonparanoid Index$_1$[6]	.30	−.44
Paranoid–Nonparanoid Index$_2$[9]	.15	−.55
Set 2		
Canonical Correlation	*1*	*2*
Goldstein-Scheerer Object-Sorting Test: [8]		
Abstraction[13]	.37	.20
Concreteness[13]	−.40	.20
Overinclusiveness[13]	.30	−.22
Idiosyncratic Responding[13]	−.08	−.23
Gorham Proverbs Test: [10]		
Abstraction[10]	.15	.90
Concreteness[10]	−.42	−.72
Autistic Responding[21]	.72	−.49
M (slope of sentence-interpretation reaction time)[3]	−.45	−.14
K (intercept of sentence-interpretation reaction time)[3]	−.32	−.16

The weighted sums for the first set corresponding to the second
canonical correlation were described by a measure of verbal IQ,[18]
years of education, drug dosage, the scale of severity of personal
illness from the Symptom–Sign Inventory,[6] and both paranoid-non-
paranoid indices. This configuration suggested a dimension of general
ability, nonparanoid status. The group of correlations for the second

set reflected a dimension of abstracting ability marked by an absence of concreteness, or autistic responding in verbal performance (proverb interpretation).

In addition to these analyses, indices of redundancy for the two canonical correlations were summed for each set of variables. The index for the first set was .19 and for the second it was .34.

Taken as a whole, the results led to the following conclusions:

1. The dimension of nonchronic paranoid status was associated with a dimension tentatively labeled rich-unusual responding.
2. The dimension of general ability, nonparanoid status was associated with one tentatively labeled semantic abstracting performance.
3. The overlap between the two sets of variables accounted for a minor proportion of variation within each set, although the proportion taken into account for the second set was considerably larger than that in the first.

REFERENCES

1. Anderson, T. W. *An introduction to multivariate statistical analysis.* New York: Wiley, 1958, p. 288.
2. Bartlett, M. S. Multivariate analysis. *J. Roy. Stat. Soc.* (Supplement), 1947, **9,** 176–197.
3. Carpenter, P. A., & Just, M. A. Sentence comprehension: A psycholinguistic processing model of verification. *Psychol. Rev.,* 1975, **82,** 45–73.
4. Cooley, W. W., & Lohnes, P. R. *Multivariate data analysis.* New York: Wiley, 1971, p. 170.
5. Dixon, W. J. (Ed.). *BMD: Biomedical computer programs.* Berkeley: University of California Press, 1973.
6. Foulds, G. A. *Personality and personal illness.* London: Tavistock, 1965.
7. Gleason, T. G. On redundancy in canonical analysis. *Psychol. Bull.,* 1976, **83,** 1004–1006.
8. Goldstein, K., & Scheerer, M. Abstract and concrete behavior: An experimental study with special tests. *Psychol. Monogr.,* Whole No. 239, 1941, **53,** 2.
9. Gordon, A. V., & Gregson, R. A. M. The symptom-sign inventory as a diagnostic differentia for paranoid and nonparanoid schizophrenics. *Brit. J. Soc. Clin. Psychol.,* 1970, **9,** 347–356.
10. Gorham, D. R. A proverbs test for clinical and experimental use. *Psychol. Reps.,* 1956, **1,** 1–12.
11. Harman, H. *Modern factor analysis.* Chicago: University of Chicago Press, 1967.

12. Harris, R. J. *A primer of multivariate statistics*. New York: Academic Press, 1975, p. 144.
13. Himmelhoch, J., Harrow, M., Tucker, G., & Hersh, J. *Manual for assessment of selected aspects of thinking: Object sorting test*. New York: Microfiche Publications, 1973, 1–25 (ASSIS/NAP No. 02206).
14. Hollingshead, A. B., & Redlich, F. C. *Social class and mental illness*. New York: Wiley, 1958.
15. Kettenring, J. R. Canonical analysis of several sets of variables. *Biometrika.*, 1971, **58**, 433–451.
16. Neufeld, R. W. J., & Broga, M. B. *Canonical correlations between diagnostic-demographic variables and indices of cognitive deficit among schizophrenic patients*. Research Bulletin No. 379, Department of Psychology, University of Western Ontario, 1976.
17. Nie, N. H., Hull, C. H., Jenkins, J. G., Steinbrenner, K., & Bent, D. H. (Eds.), *Statistical package for the social sciences*. New York: McGraw-Hill, 1970.
18. Paitich, D., & Crawford, G. *A multiple-choice version of the WAIS Vocabulary*. Unpublished manuscript, Clarke Institute of Psychiatry, Toronto, 1970.
19. Pilowsky, I., Leine, S., & Boulton, D. M. The classification of depression by numerical taxonomy. *Brit. J. Psychiat.*, 1969, **115**, 937–45.
20. Seligman, M. E. P. *Helplessness: On depression, development and death*. San Francisco: Freeman, 1975.
21. Shimkunas, A. M., Gynther, M. D., & Smith, K. *Scoring manual for autistic responses to the Gorham Proverbs Test*. Unpublished manuscript, Washington University School of Medicine, 1967.
22. Stewart, D. K., & Love, W. A. A general canonical correlation index. *Psychol. Bull.*, 1968, **70**, 160–163.
23. Weckowicz, T. E., Muir, W., & Cropley, A. J. A factor analysis of the beck inventory of depression. *J. Consult. Psychol.*, 1967, **31**, 23–28.

10

Introduction to Empirical Classification Approaches

PRELIMINARY CONSIDERATIONS

The procedures presented in the last two chapters are concerned with data variance which is constrained in some way to external criteria. In the case of multiple regression the criterion consists of a designated variable to be predicted. The variables serving as the predictors are weighted according to the constraint of maximal correspondence between the composite predictor scores and values of the designated variable. In the case of discriminant-function analysis, the criterion consists of categorical classes, and the weights for the predictors are designed to meet the requirement of maximum separation of the classes. Canonical correlation is concerned with the variation and covariation in one set of variables as it relates to the variation and covariation of the alternate set. Unlike these methods, empirical classification approaches are concerned with the most pronounced aspects of variation in the sample of data without any immediate, external constraints. The aim is to identify the most pronounced aspects of systematic variation in the sample in order to reduce the description of intersubject differences to a manageable number of representative data profiles. The term profile analysis is often used to describe this process.

Consider the clinician confronting a large pool of subject data relating to patients' dispositions at admission to a treatment institution. These variables include a mixture of demographic and diagnostic indices along with results from psychometric tests. If the data profiles from one hundred admissions are available, the clinician will want to pare it down to some meaningful discription of the information available in the total pool. The main considerations underlying this enterprise are relatively straightforward.

For one hundred profiles, it is probable that very few, if any, will be absolutely identical. Thus, for one hundred patients, there are conceivably one hundred unique profiles. Part of our goal is to identify their most pronounced aspects of difference. Conversely, for one hundred profiles, there are probably not two that are completely devoid of any common characteristics. So a second aspect of our aim is to ascertain the most pronounced components of overlap among them. Our twofold goal consequently is to isolate the main similarities and differences among the profiles in our original set. We can begin by analyzing the data to obtain several "characteristic profiles." Each characteristic profile should be representative of a subset of patients in the sample, but unrepresentative of the patients typified by the remaining profiles. In this sense, the redundancy of information among all the initial profiles, taken together, is markedly condensed. The subsets of patients represented by the respective characteristic profiles are sometimes referred to as clusters, and the inquiry itself called cluster analysis.

The characteristic profiles are interpreted as types or classes of patients in the initial sample. If these profiles reliably appear when analyses are performed on other samples, they can be used to characterize the profiles of incoming patients. The new patient can be classified according to the characteristic profile which most closely resembles his own. In this way, a classification system based on the replicable characteristic profiles is developed, having been derived from the distinctive types of presenting profiles among previous samples. This profile-oriented classifying procedure is considered empirical inasmuch as it depends solely on the presenting configurations of data, rather than on some theoretical framework or preexisting system based on clinical judgment.

Profile (or cluster) analysis is therefore concerned with searching out the most salient aspects of data variation. The resulting profiles are likely to be more reliable than if some other criterion were used. However, when considering this criterion, one must remember the reasons for engaging in classification in the first place—mainly, treatment implication and prognostic significance. A tacit assumption of this approach is that the most pronounced aspects of data-profile variation are likely to bear the most meaningful relationship to these two aspects of the clinical enterprise. This assumption is circumvented by other methods of data analysis which focus only on the aspects of data variation directly related to the criterion indices of prognosis and/or treatment efficacy at the outset.

Another use of characteristic profiles is to obtain suggestive information regarding etiological factors of various syndromes. Again, we assume that the most pronounced forms of profile variation are likely to be the vital ones regarding the manifestation of etiological factors. For these profiles to have practical relevance, they must consist of measures that are linked to etiology. Furthermore, the etiological factors should produce systematic variation in the data which is strong enough to be detected by profile-analytic methods. To illustrate, suppose that an etiological factor in endogenous depression consists of a deficit of norepinephrine in certain neuroanatomical sites. An analysis of a number of physiological measures from depressed and other psychiatric patients will point up this etiological factor only if it produces a pattern of variation which is known to be symptomatic of the norepinephrine deficit. If irrelevant measures are used, or if the configuration of relevant measures is only slightly affected by the etiological factor, the resulting profiles are helpless to provide information about the source of the syndrome.

The use of empirical classification procedures present a number of continuing difficulties which center in large part on problems of profile instability. The results of profile analysis can be unreliable with changes in subject samples;[10] variation in preparation of the data (such as the introduction of different transformations before submitting it to the analysis[17]); and inconsistencies in cluster analysis procedures.[1] Variations in cluster analysis procedures include such factors as differences in criteria for what constitutes similarity between profiles; whether or not greater emphasis is placed on similarity within clusters or dissimilarity between clusters; or the number of groups to be formed at different stages of clustering. For classification based on empirical methods to be successful, the referent profiles must be fairly robust, at least with respect to the introduction of new samples.[10]

Because of the problems such as those cited, many clinicians avoid these methods of classification. Their apprehension is intensified by the apparent complexity of the mathematical and computational requirements. Part of this difficulty can be mastered by a few basic concepts to be discussed here; and since most of the computer programs for these methods are publicly available, computational difficulties are easily overcome. On the other hand, avoiding these procedures because they give results of less than the desired degree of reliability does not eliminate the need to extract information from a large pool of data. Dealing with this problem cannot be postponed until perfect methodological procedures are created. The methods of empirical classification currently available incorporate the best procedures developed to date. It makes little sense to adopt less efficient procedures, or to abandon the problem altogether.

BASIC APPROACHES TO PROFILE ANALYSIS

There are two main aspects of profile analysis underlying the majority of formal procedures. The first involves the method of quantifying commonality between any two profiles; the second is the approach taken in analyzing the commonality estimates, to obtain profiles that best represent the systematic modes of variation within the sample. There has been a proliferation of different versions of profile analysis with accompanying computer programs.[1,9,10,16] The main concern of each, however, is essentially to optimize methods of estimating inter-profile commonality and to analyze these estimates to maximize clustering solutions.

There are usually two methods of quantifying profile similarity. The first computes the index distance squared, or D^2. Consider data profiles for N subjects with p measures each. Let the value for the qth measure on the ith subject be denoted x_{iq}. The estimate of D^2 between any two subjects, i and j, would be obtained as:

$$D_{ij}^2 = \sum_{q=1}^{p} (x_{iq} - x_{jq})^2$$

If the p measures are arranged in the form of a p-tuple vector with that for the ith subject designated $\mathbf{x}_i$ and that for the jth subject designated $\mathbf{x}_j$, then D_{ij}^2 in vector notation becomes $(\mathbf{x}_i - \mathbf{x}_j)'(\mathbf{x}_i - \mathbf{x}_j)$.

It may be helpful to consider a graphical representation of D_{ij} as depicted in Figure A-3 (page 170). For convenience, p is only 3. The axes X_1, X_2, and X_3 represent the measures entered into the threefold profile. The projections of the vectors $\mathbf{x}_i$ and $\mathbf{x}_j$ onto these axes represent the values of the measures for subjects i and j. The value of D_{ij} equals the square root of the sum of the squared differences in these projections:

$$\left[\sum_{q=1}^{p}(x_{iq}-x_{jq})^2\right]^{1/2}$$

Where $p = 2$, the distance between the subjects defined by their two vectors is simply a case in point of the hypotenuse of a right-angled triangle. The value of D_{ij}^2 is actually an index of profile *dissimilarity* because as it increases, the similarity between the two profiles decreases. For D^2 to represent a meaningful index of dissimilarity, the p measures must have uniform dispersions (standard deviations) over the subjects in the sample—unless the investigator wishes to weight the contributions of the various measures to the D^2 index in proportion to their dispersions.

The other, less commonly used measure of inter-profile relationship, is known as the vector-product index. The vector-product index is the sum of the cross-product between the respective measures for a pair of subjects, or:

$$\sum_{q=1}^{p}x_{iq}x_{jq}$$

In vector notation, this value is $\mathbf{x}'_i\mathbf{x}_j$. The vector product reflects the projection of one vector onto the other. Where the vectors have not been normalized—that is, where their lengths do not equal one (see Appendix A)—the vector product corresponds to the length of the projection of one of the vectors onto the other, times the length of the other. If the vectors have been normalized, the vector product is equal to the length of the projection of one of the vectors onto the other. In Figure A-3, the vector $\mathbf{r}$ represents the projection of $\mathbf{x}_i$ onto $\mathbf{x}_j$. This projection is defined as $(\mathbf{x}'_i\mathbf{x}_j)\mathbf{x}_j$. If $(\mathbf{x}'_i\mathbf{x}_j)$ is designated c_{ij}, then the length of r becomes $c_{ij}(\mathbf{x}'_j\mathbf{x}_j)^{1/2}$. As the bracketed term is now equal to one, the length of $\mathbf{r}$ equals c_{ij}, or the vector product between subject profiles i and j. Normalization of profiles prior to computing vector products is important both for enhancing the conceptual clarity of the cross-products index, and for equalizing the values for different pairs of identical profiles. As Overall and Klett[10] point out, where the profiles are not first normalized, two pairs of identical profiles can have different vector-product values if the pairs differ in length. Since our concern is with profile similarity, equally similar pairs of profiles should have identical vector-product values.

It is not uncommon for investigators to eliminate the influence of individual differences in the mean values of the profile measures on the similarity index. This is typically known as elimination of differences in profile elevation and can easily be accomplished by subtracting from each subject's profile the mean of all p measures from the individual scores on the p measures. (It is assumed at the outset that the measures have similar variances over subjects; if not, they should immediately be made similar through conversion to Z scores using the mean and standard deviations computed over the N subjects.) The vector product becomes the sum of the cross-products of the p deviation scores, or:

$$\sum_{q=1}^{p} (x_{iq} - \bar{x}_i.)(x_{jq} - \bar{x}_j.).$$

The square of the length of the deviation-score vector for subject i is:

$$\sum_{q=1}^{p} (x_{iq} - \bar{x}_i.)^2$$

This value is equal to $p\sigma_i^2$, where σ_i^2 is the variance of the p measures for subject i. In order to normalize the difference-score vector, each of the p deviation scores must be multiplied by $1/(p\sigma_i^2)^{1/2}$. As the profile for the jth subject is similarly normalized, the vector product now becomes

$$\sum_{q=1}^{p} (x_{iq} - \bar{x}_i.)(x_{jq} - \bar{x}_j.)/p\sigma_i\sigma_j$$

which is the formula for the coefficient of correlation between the profiles of subjects i and j. Hence, a commonly used index of profile similarity is Pearson's r. The preceding development shows that if profile elevations are equalized and the resulting vectors normalized, variances (known as profile scatter) are also equalized. With elevation and scatter equalized, the only profile parameter remaining to influence the size of the similarity index is profile shape. This parameter refers to the scores of the p measures relative to one another. Hence, when the correlation coefficient is used as the index of profile communality, the investigator is typically interested only in profile similarity with respect to the interrelationships among the measures, and not to similarity in the measures' absolute values or the inter-measure variance.

For a sample of N subjects, there will be $\frac{1}{2}(N)(N-1)$ unique pairs, and hence $\frac{1}{2}(N)(N-1)$ profile-similarity values. The next phase of the procedure consists in using these values to identify the systematic individual differences, the characteristic profiles, in the sample. Using D^2 as the relationship index, Sawrey, Keller, and Conger[13] outlined a series of steps for constructing groups of subjects homogeneous to each other but different in relation to those in opposite groups.

A less laborious method which probably gives similar results has been presented by Overall and Klett.[10] An N by N matrix of D^2 values is first constructed. The element in the ith row and jth column is the D^2 value for subject pair ij, or D_{ij}^2. A nucleus group of three subjects is then formed. To select this group, columns of the D^2 matrix are scanned to find the individual who has two other individuals highly similar to himself. The column with a pair of D^2 values whose average is smaller than the pair in any other column is identified. The nucleus group is thus made up of the individual corresponding to that column along with the two individuals with the least average D^2 values in the column. For each of the remaining ($N-3$) individuals, the following ratios are calculated: the average D^2 between the individuals in the nucleus group, and the average D^2 between the individuals not in the nucleus group. Overall and Klett term this ratio the "ratio of cluster-to-noncluster distances." The next candidate included in the group is the remaining individual with the smallest ratio of cluster to noncluster distances—provided that his ratio is not above some critical value. This value is arbitrary and can vary according to the strictness of cluster-group homogeneity. Overall and Klett point out that a typical value is .6. After the new candidate is added, cluster to noncluster distances for the remaining members are calculated using the now expanded cluster group and the diminished remaining group. This process is continued until none of the ratios for the remaining subjects are below the set criterion. Addition to the existing cluster is at this point discontinued, and new clusters are sought. Initiation of a new cluster employs the same procedures as for the existing cluster, but only considers individuals remaining outside the existing cluster. Addition to the new cluster proceeds along the same lines as addition to the earlier cluster, until the criterion ratio is not met, when still another cluster is sought. This operation of cluster formation continues until the criterion ratio can no longer be met by any of the remaining profiles. When the analysis is complete, the nature of the profiles represented by each cluster can be estimated as the p means for the p measures, each mean taken over the members of the cluster. This set of means is known as the cluser's centroid.

It is apparent that cluster analysis methods such as this one involve considerable computational labor. Computer programs such as those of Overall and Klett[10] and Veldman[19] make these methods more feasible.

To identify characteristic profiles when the vector-product index of communality is used, we proceed in a similar manner as for D^2. An N by N matrix of vector product values is formed. The element in the ith row and j^{th} column of the matrix consists of the vector product between subjects i and j. This procedure was originated by Holzinger and Harman,[6] who applied it to the vector-products of normalized deviation-score profiles, or the correlation coefficients between profile pairs. The correlation is traditionally termed a Q-type correlation, and as mentioned, removes the influence of elevation and scatter on the vector products. The initial nucleus-group pair consists of the two subjects with the largest vector product. Next, the profile among those subjects remaining with the highest average vector-product between itself and those currently in the cluster, relative to the average vector-product between itself and the other remaining profiles, is identified and added to the cluster. Again, a restriction for addition is that the ratio must meet some criterion value—in this case, the ratio must *exceed* the criterion. The criterion value is arbitrarily chosen (for example, 1.3).[10] After adding the acceptable candidate, the diminished number of individuals remaining are considered for possible addition to the cluster. The one with the highest ratio of averaged cluster to noncluster vector products is added, provided that the minimum-ratio criterion is satisfied. The process continues until the criterion cannot be satisfied, and is then repeated from the beginning for the remaining unclustered individuals. The process is reiterated until the minimum-ratio criterion can no longer be met for any new cluster formation.

One difficulty with the cluster procedures outlined thus far involves the effects of averaging the communality indexes over the unclustered individuals. Overall and Klett[10] cogently pointed out that the candidate under consideration for cluster inclusion may have low D^2 values in relation to a small subset of remaining individuals. The average D^2 between the candidate and its subset may in fact be smaller than the average D^2 between the candidate and the clustered individuals. However, when the totality of the remaining individuals are taken into the computation, the average D^2 may be inflated by those individuals who are dissimilar to the candidate, in which case the cluster to noncluster ratio as initially defined will meet the criterion value and include the candidate in the existing cluster. Similar considerations apply when vector-products are used as the index of commonality. The clustering methods for D^2 presented by Sawrey, Keller, and Conger[13] overcome this problem to some extent because averaging procedures are not used in the early stages of group formation. A modification of the present procedural framework was used by Overall and Klett. It applies to either D^2 or vector-product matrices, and consists of basing the noncluster part of the cluster-to-noncluster ratio on the average values between the candidate and any other triad of remaining individuals. Instead of considering the remaining contingent in its entirety, this modification allows for the possibility of a more appropriate cluster nested within the unclustered remainder. Triads of the remaining contingent are used because a cluster is deemed to require a sample of at least three individuals.

The use of factor analytic methods is a different approach to analyzing vector-product matrices. Many excellent sources for factor analysis are available, including the classic ones by Harman[4] and by Horst,[7] as well as more recent treatments for social scientists such as Van de Geer[18] Cooley and Lohnes,[3] Overall and Klett,[10] and Harris.[5*] This approach has been gaining in popularity and, as Overall and Klett[10] pointed out, is likely to enhance the reliability of the characteristic profiles because they are based on a solution which takes all profiles of the sample into account collectively, rather than in sequence. In addition, the obtained characteristic profiles successively maximize the residual variance accounted for in the matrix of vector-products after the variance given by the preceding profiles has been removed (See Appendix C, page 183). Basically, the factor analytic approach derives the N latent vectors (see Appendix B) of the N by N matrix of vector products. After normalizing the latent vectors to their latent roots (see Appendix B), the original N by N matrix of vector products can be reproduced by postmultiplying the matrix of latent vectors by its transpose. However, the original matrix can usually be closely approximated by using a matrix with sizeably fewer than N latent vectors. Typically, only the first m latent vectors

---

* A thorough treatment of factor analytic methods is beyond the intended scope of this book. However, a general description of the method as applied to profile vector-product matrices, with reference to the vector and matrix algebra in Appendices A and B, will be undertaken. The reader wishing to adopt this approach to profile analysis can refer to the work of Overall and Klett[10] and the recent developments of Modal Profile Analysis emanating from Jackson's laboratory.[14,15]

constitute the columns of this matrix, where the remaining $(N - m)$ latent vectors only slightly improve the fit of the reproduced N by N matrix of vector products to the original N by N matrix. The essential configuration of the original N by N matrix of profile interrelationships is encapsulated in the retained m latent vectors. In this sense, the profile types corresponding to the first m latent vectors represent the characteristic profiles in the sample. The ith coordinate of a given latent vector is the degree to which the profile of subject i corresponds to the characteristic profile represented by the latent vector.

The obtained latent profiles can be rotated according to some criterion such as varimax. The varimax rotation allows each rotated characteristic profile to represent a subsample of profiles to a greater extent than its unrotated counterpart. In rotating the latent vectors, the configuration of inter-subject relations, as defined by the vector products, is in no way violated. The rotation simply affords a more easily interpreted description of these interrelationships.

Clusters can be formed by assigning each individual to the profile cluster of his highest latent-vector coordinate, provided that it meets some arbitrary minimum-criterion value (.5 where Q-correlations form the vector products). Thus, the cluster corresponding to a given characteristic profile (latent vector) consists of all individuals having their largest coordinate value for that vector and meeting the criterion of minimum coordinate value.

Each individual's profile will bear some resemblance to each characteristic profile according to the size of the corresponding latent-vector coordinate. Thus, instead of assigning the individual to one of the profile clusters, he could be described in terms of the relative sizes of his relationships to the m profile clusters.

We have dealt with the latent-vector coordinates that denote the correspondence of subjects' profiles to the characteristic profiles without taking into account the nature of the characteristic profiles themselves. Their description is obtained by carrying out the following operations. The N by p matrix of original profiles (where the ith row corresponds to scores on the p measures for subject i) is premultiplied by the transpose of the N by m matrix of latent vectors (see Appendix B). This product represents the m by p matrix of characteristic profiles, each row corresponding to one of the characteristic profiles. These characteristic profiles are independent of one another in the sense that they are uncorrelated. In other words, the p scores for each profile are not predictable from the p scores of another profile.

The classification of new patients is relatively straight forward.

One simply obtains the correlations between the patient's profile and the m characteristic profiles in the m by p matrix previously described. These values will be proportional to the correspondence between the new patient's profile and the m characteristic profiles. He can be described according to the profile maximally correlating with his own; or, he can be described according to his correspondence to the m characteristic profiles using the m correlations.

Recent developments in the factor analytic approach to profile analysis include those presented by Jackson and his students.[14,15] "Modal Profiles" are obtained to enhance the reliability of the obtained profiles. The initial sample is divided into two or more subsamples at the outset. Separate analyses are carried out on each of the resulting subsample matrices of vector products. After a second-order analysis on the characteristic profiles emerging from each of the subsamples, modal profiles are obtained. These are derived through a method of weighting the initial characteristic profiles for each subgroup according to the degree of overlap with those obtained from the opposite subgroups. Thus, an effort is made to protect against the error of seriously entertaining characteristic profiles that are unstable at the start.

EXAMPLES OF EMPIRICAL CLASSIFICATION IN THE CLINICAL SETTING

In recent years, an increasing number of studies have been designed to develop taxonomies of behavioral disorder, based on empirical clusters of data profiles. Individual studies tend to use their own modifications of the procedures already outlined. The features of each of those studies will not be reviewed in detail here. This section is intended to give an idea of the outcomes from a sample of studies on empirical classification. Interested readers can refer to the original sources for details of the studies they wish to pursue further. It is unfortunate that certain aspects of the procedures for each study have been somewhat unique. Blashfield[1] pointed out that the resulting profiles can be sensitive to different nuances in procedure. The reader should not expect robust results of empirical classificatory methods when ensuing analyses markedly depart from the analytical methods used in the initial profile derivations.

Carlson[2] carried out a study concerned with an empirical taxonomy of subjects in correctional institutions. His measures consisted of the fifteen subscales of the Differential Personality Inventory,[8] and his subjects were a mixture of 287 individuals from five correctional institutions, in addition to one hundred university undergraduates. The university students were included to facilitate the identification of offender-specific characteristic profiles. In the first phase, a matrix of vector products (Q-correlations) was used to form clusters on the basis of profile shape. In the second phase, a distance index was used to further subdivide clusters, which were now similar in profile shape, according to profile elevation and scatter. In addition, a series of checks on the obtained clusters were carried out: cross-validation by a technique of splitting the total sample into two subsamples; cross-validation using a different set of measures—self-ratings on a number of demographic and "criminal career" related questions; and testing the adequacy of cluster-group separation using discriminant-function analysis (see chapter 8). With these analytical methods and criteria for profile reliability, Carlson isolated twelve stable profiles. Moreover, those clustered according to the Differential Personality Inventory data differed in a number of other variables including age, education, and socioeconomic background; and on several of the self-report rating questions including aggressiveness, sexual activity, and certain criminal-record items. Surprisingly, a large number of university students were allocated to clusters that contained a sizable number of criminals. In some respects, the similarities of criminal and noncriminal profiles may outweigh the differences.

Another study using empirical classificatory procedures was made by Paykel,[11] addressing the taxonomy of depressed patients. Paykel's measures were six factor scores[4] (see footnote, page 133, chapter 8) based on a factor analysis of thirty-five original measures, including clinical symptom ratings, demographic data, and psychometric measures. The factor scores reflected dimensions such as "general severity of depression" and "psychotic versus neurotic depression." Subjects were 165 depressed patients from several treatment settings. The clustering methods were somewhat different from those previously discussed in this chapter. They were essentially a variation on the D^2 approach. Basically, the clustering criterion consisted of arranging groups of subjects so that the distances between the members of the group and the group centroid (the group means on the six factor scores) relative to the distances between group centroids, were minimized. Four clusters were obtained. The corresponding profiles indicated that they represented: psychotic depression including high severity with some delusional trends and good premorbid adjustment; moderate depression marked by anxiety and high neuroticism scores; depression with intermixed hostility; and mild depression associated with personality disorder. The inherent parsimony in paring down the information from 165 profiles to four representative profiles is apparent, illustrating the clinical advantages available in such methods.

In an ingenious study by Price and Moos[12] a different sort of entity was the object of classification. The investigators sought to identify systematic differences in the profiles of treatment milieus rather than in the profiles of patients. They rated psychiatric treatment wards on ten scales taken from Moos' Ward Atmosphere Scale. These scales measured the domains of staff and patient interaction; treatment program philosophy; and administrative structure or systems maintenance. Using ratings on these scales from patients and staff, profiles were obtained for 144 treatment programs. The index of inter-profile communality was a vector product that maintained similarities in profile elevation. From the 144 treatment programs, six characteristic profiles emerged: "Therapeutic Community Programs, Relationship-Oriented Programs, Action-Oriented Programs, Insight-Oriented Programs, Control-Oriented Programs, and Disturbed Behavior Programs." There were three notable external correlates of these profiles. The first was the institutions with which they tended to be affiliated. The Veterans Administration centers in the study had no therapeutic community programs—action-oriented programs, which emphasize patient self-management and decision making, and insight-oriented programs were associated with state hospitals. The second correlate was absolute number of patients, control-oriented programs having the most and action-oriented programs the least. The third was the patient to staff ratios. The largest was found for the action-oriented programs and the smallest for the disturbed-behavior programs.

The last study we will mention here was on alcoholic personality types by Skinner, Jackson, and Hoffman.[14] As in the study by Carlson, the subscales of the Differential Personality Inventory formed the profile measures. The investigators used the method of Modal Profile Analysis based on factor-analytic methods. The index of inter-subject profile communality was the Q-correlation coefficient. Three subsamples were formed for cross-validation purposes before the actual analysis. Characteristic profiles based on factor analysis were first obtained from each of the three subsamples. Modal Profiles were then derived by combining the initial profiles according to weights reflecting their stability over the alternate subgroups. Five clearly interpretable Modal Profiles were identified. Their descriptions came from the profiles of subjects having both high negative and high positive values on the Modal Profile latent vectors of subject coordinates. They were labeled: "Acute Anxiety versus Denial and Blunted Affect; Antisocial Attitudes versus Hypochondriacal Preoccupation; Hostile-Hallucinatory Syndrome versus Neurotic Depression; Neurotic Disorganization versus Hostile-Paranoid; and Emotional Instability versus Interpersonal Conflict and Depression." Those profiles with high negative values on the vectors of subject coordinates defined different groups from those with high positive values, but only one Modal Profile was considered necessary to describe both groups. The profiles of those with high negative subject coordinates were reflections (the inverses) of the profiles of those with high positive subject coordinates on the same vectors.

REFERENCES

1. Blashfield, R. K. Mixture model tests of cluster analysis: Accuracy of four agglomerative hierarchical methods. *Psychol. Bull.*, 1976, **83**, 377–388.
2. Carlson, K. A. Classes of adult offenders. *J. Abn. Psychol.*, 1972, **79**, 84–93.
3. Cooley, W. W., & Lohnes, P. R. *Multivariate data analysis*. New York: Wiley, 1971.
4. Harman, H. H. *Modern factor analysis* (2nd ed.). Chicago: University of Chicago Press, 1967.
5. Harris, R. J. *A primer of multivariate statistics*. New York: Academic Press, 1975.
6. Holzinger, K. J., & Harman, H. H. *Factor analysis*. Chicago: University of Chicago Press, 1941.
7. Horst, P. *Factor analysis of data matrices*. New York: Holt, Rinehart & Winston, 1965.
8. Jackson, D. N., & Messick, S. Response styles and the assessment of psychopathology. In S. Messick & J. Ross (Eds.), *Measurement in personality and cognition*. New York: Wiley, 1962.
9. Overall, J. E. Configural analysis of diagnostic stereotypes. *Behav. Sci.*, 1963, **8**, 211–219.
10. Overall, J. E., & Klett, C. J. *Applied multivariate analysis*. New York: McGraw-Hill, 1972, p. 180.
11. Paykel, E. S. Classification of depressed patients: A cluster analysis derived grouping. *Br. J. Psychiat.*, 1971, **118**, 275–288.
12. Price, R. H., & Moos, R. H. Toward a taxonomy of inpatient treatment environments. *J. Abn. Psychol.*, 1975, **84**, 181–188.

13. Sawrey, W. L., Keller, L., & Conger, J. J. An objective method of grouping profiles by distance functions and its relation to factor analysis. *Educ. Psychol. Meas.*, 1960, **20**, 651–673.
14. Skinner, H. A., Jackson, D. N., & Hoffman, H. Alcoholic personality types: Identification and correlates. *J. Abn. Psychol.*, 1974, **83**, 658–666.
15. Skinner, H. A., Reed, P. L., & Jackson, D. N. Toward the objective diagnosis of psychopathology: Generalizability of modal personality profiles. *J. Consult. Clin. Psychol.*, 1976, **44**, 111–117.
16. Sneath, H. A., & Sokal, R. R. *Numerical taxonomy*. San Francisco: Freeman, 1973.
17. Strauss, J. S., Bartko, J. J., & Carpenter, W. J. The use of clustering techniques for the classification of psychiatric patients. *Br. J. Psychiat.*, 1973, **122**, 531–540.
18. Van de Geer, J. P. *Introduction to multivariate statistics for the social sciences*. San Francisco: Freeman, 1971.
19. Veldman, D. J. *Fortran programming for the behavioral sciences*. New York: Holt, Rinehart & Winston, 1967.

Appendix A
Some Basic Vector Calculations

GENERAL DESCRIPTION

A vector is an ordered series of real numbers referring to several reference axes. The real numbers are the projections of a point defined by the vector on these axes. The number of referent axes is denoted p. A vector is schematically conceptualized in Figure A-1. The vector, denoted in bold face, $\mathbf{x}_i$, represents a point defined by three axes x_1, x_2, and x_p, where in this case $p = 3$. The subscript i distinguishes the point referring to entity i. The projections $x_{iq}(q = 1, 2, \ldots, p)$ define the location of the point with respect to the p axes. In practice, if the point is a subject, the axes correspond to p measures on the subject (such as age, education and IQ) and the size of the projections represent the values of these measures for the subject. The entity can also represent a measure such as IQ. The axes would then correspond to three subjects and the projections would designate the IQs for the respective subjects. We refer to the projections as the coordinates of the vector with respect to the referent axes.

The vector coordinates are arranged in a column, proceeding in order from the projection onto the first axis to the pth axis:

$$\mathbf{x}_i = \begin{pmatrix} x_{i1} \\ x_{i2} \\ x_{i3} \\ \vdots \\ x_{ip} \end{pmatrix} \text{for example} \begin{pmatrix} 3 \\ 2 \\ -4 \\ \vdots \\ 10 \end{pmatrix}$$

Where $p = 3$, the vector consists of the three corresponding coordinates. The coordinates must be *ordered* so that there is no ambiguity as to which axis they designate. The set of values constituting the vector is referred to as a p-tuple set of real numbers, and the vector as a p-tuple vector. Hence, a 3-tuple would be a triple, a 4-tuple a quadruple, and so on. The locus of intersection of the referent axes—the point at which they meet in Figure A-1—is designated zero. The coordinates for the vector can be positive or negative depending on the direction of the projections onto the axes.

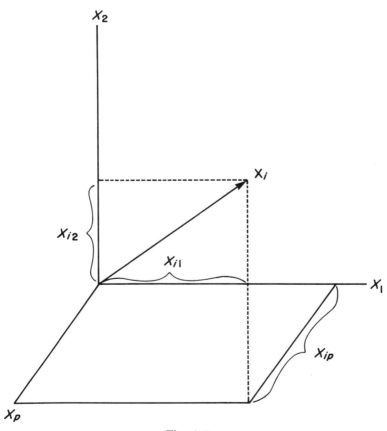

Fig. A-1.

Vector Subtraction and Addition

One vector $\mathbf{x}_i$ can be subtracted from another vector $\mathbf{x}_j$, by subtracting each of the coordinates of $\mathbf{x}_i$ from the corresponding coordinates of $\mathbf{x}_j$:

$$\mathbf{x}_j - \mathbf{x}_i = \begin{pmatrix} x_{j1} \\ x_{j2} \\ x_{j3} \\ \vdots \\ x_{jp} \end{pmatrix} - \begin{pmatrix} x_{i1} \\ x_{i2} \\ x_{i3} \\ \vdots \\ x_{ip} \end{pmatrix} = \begin{pmatrix} x_{j1} - x_{i1} \\ x_{j2} - x_{i2} \\ x_{j3} - x_{i3} \\ \vdots \\ x_{jp} - x_{i3} \end{pmatrix}$$

For example, if $\mathbf{x}_j$ were the 4-tuple vector $\begin{pmatrix} 5 \\ 4 \\ 8 \\ 1 \end{pmatrix}$ and $\mathbf{x}_i$ were $\begin{pmatrix} 5 \\ 3 \\ 7 \\ 6 \end{pmatrix}$

$\mathbf{x}_j - \mathbf{x}_i$ would be $\begin{pmatrix} 0 \\ 1 \\ 1 \\ -5 \end{pmatrix}$

In a similar manner, the addition of vectors $\mathbf{x}_j$ and $\mathbf{x}_i$ involves the addition of their corresponding coordinates. In addition, the new vector consists of the coordinate sums. In subtraction, a new vector is formed with coordinates consisting of the difference values. Figure A-2 schematically depicts the operation of subtracting one 2-tuple vector from another. Here, $\mathbf{x}_j - \mathbf{x}_i$ results in the residual vector $\mathbf{x}_s$. The coordinates for $\mathbf{x}_s$, x_{s1}, and x_{s2} correspond to $x_{j1} - x_{i1}$ and $x_{j2} - x_{i2}$ respectively.

With reference to addition, vector $\mathbf{x}_j$ is the sum of vectors $\mathbf{x}_i$ and $\mathbf{x}_s$. This can be schematically conceptualized where the vector $\mathbf{x}_j$ is defined as the point located by translating vector $\mathbf{x}_s$ so that it emanates from the point defined by $\mathbf{x}_i$, in effect adding $\mathbf{x}_s$ to $\mathbf{x}_i$ after locating $\mathbf{x}_i$ in the 2-axis space.

Multiplication of Vectors

To multiply one vector by another, each coordinate of the first is multiplied by the corresponding coordinate of the second and the products are then summed:

$$\sum_{q=1}^{p} x_{iq} x_{jq}$$

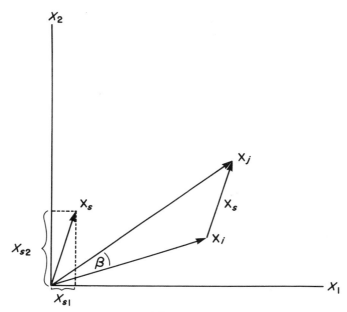

Fig. A-2.

The product between vectors x_i and x_j is written $x_i'x_j$. The prime following x_i denotes its *transpose*; the transpose of a vector simply means that its coordinates appear in order as a row of values rather than as a column: $x_i' = (x_{i1}, x_{i2}, x_{i3}, \ldots, x_{ip})$. The importance of designating the product of two vectors as the transpose of the first times the second in column form will become apparent in the discussion of matrix calculations in Appendix B. Multiplying a vector by itself is designated as its "inner product," the inner product of vector x_i being $x_i'x_i$. This value corresponds to the sum of the squared values of its coordinates.

The length of a vector, its *norm*, is derived from the vector's inner product. The norm is equal to the square root of the sum of the vector's coordinates squared:

$$\left(\sum_{q=1}^{p} x_{iq}^2 \right)^{1/2}$$, which is equal to the square root of its inner product, $(x_i'x_i)^{1/2}$.

Suppose a 3-tuple vector x_i was $\begin{pmatrix} 3 \\ 1 \\ 2 \end{pmatrix}$ and a 3-tuple vector, x_j, was $\begin{pmatrix} 4 \\ 2 \\ 3 \end{pmatrix}$.

Then $\mathbf{x}_i'\mathbf{x}_j$ would be $(3, 1, 2) \cdot \begin{pmatrix} 4 \\ 2 \\ 3 \end{pmatrix}$

$= (3)(4) + (1)(2) + (2)(3) = 20$; the norm of $\mathbf{x}_i$ would be $(\mathbf{x}_i'\mathbf{x}_i)^{1/2}$

$= \left[(3, 1, 2). \begin{pmatrix} 3 \\ 1 \\ 2 \end{pmatrix} \right]^{1/2}$

$= 14^{1/2} = 3.74$; the norm of $\mathbf{x}_j$ would be $\left[(4, 2, 3). \begin{pmatrix} 4 \\ 2 \\ 3 \end{pmatrix} \right]^{1/2}$

$= 29^{1/2} = 5.38$.

If a vector is multiplied by a constant c, called a *scalar*, the product consists of a vector whose coordinates are those of the original vector, each multiplied by the scalar. For the vector $\mathbf{x}_i$ multiplied by the scalar c, the product would be

$$\begin{pmatrix} cx_{i1} \\ cx_{i2} \\ cx_{i3} \\ \vdots \\ cx_{ip} \end{pmatrix}$$

The product obtained in this fashion is simply an extension of, or a portion of, the original vector. If the scalar is greater than one, the product becomes an extended form of the original vector—that is, the original vector but with greater length: If the scalar is less than one, the product is the original vector but with reduced length.

A certain kind of scalar becomes important when the norms of a series of vectors are to be equalized. It is common to scale each vector so that its norm is equal to one. In this case, the scalar becomes the reciprocal of its norm. For example, multiplying $\mathbf{x}_i$ in the preceding example by the reciprocal of its norm of 3.74 would lead to the following coordinates:

$$1/3.74 \begin{pmatrix} 3 \\ 1 \\ 2 \end{pmatrix} = \begin{pmatrix} .802 \\ .267 \\ .535 \end{pmatrix}$$

The value of $(1/3.74\ \mathbf{x}_i)'(1/3.74\ \mathbf{x}_i)$ is now equal to 1, the square root of which is 1; the vector $\mathbf{x}_i$ is said to have been "normalized."

PROJECTIONS OF VECTORS ONTO EACH OTHER, AND
DISTANCES BETWEEN THEM

The product between two vectors is equal to the length of the projection of one of the vectors onto the other, times the norm of the other. The projection of a vector x_i onto x_j is represented in Figure A-3 as the vector r. This projection is obtained as the point on x_j corresponding to the line connecting x_i and x_j, 90 degrees to x_j. The vector r is defined as $(x_i'x_j)x_j$. Similarly, the projection of x_j onto x_i would be defined as $(x_i'x_j)x_i$. If x_j were normalized, the vector product would be equal to the length of the projection of x_i onto x_j— that is, the length of r would be simply $x_i'x_j$. We can illustrate this projection by considering the norm of r. Since r is defined as x_j scaled by the value of the vector product $x_i'x_j$, the norm of r is equal to $[(x_i'x_j)^2(x_j'x_j)]^{1/2}$. Since x_j has been normalized, $x_j'x_j$ is equal to 1, and hence, the norm of r is equal to $x_i'x_j$.

When the projection of one vector onto another is zero, the vectors are said to be *orthogonal* to one another. Schematically, orthogonal vectors are those that define a 90-degree angle. In this case, their vector product would also be zero. The referent axes in Figures A-1, A-2, and A-3 can be considered as cases in point of orthogonal vectors. The vectors x_i and x_j in Figure A-2 are not orthogonal because their angle of separation, β, is less than 90 degrees.

The distance between two vectors is the square root of the sum of the differences between their corresponding coordinates squared:

$$D_{ij} = \left[\sum_{q=1}^{p} (x_{jq} - x_{iq})^2 \right]^{1/2} \text{ or } [(x_j - x_i)'(x_j - x_i)]^{1/2}$$

The distance D_{ij} is depicted in Figure A-3, and in Figure A-2 as the vector x_s translated onto the end of vector x_i. The norm of vector x_s corresponds to D_{ij} since its coordinates are the differences between the coordinates of x_i and x_j.

The first formula for D_{ij} given above can be expanded:

$$D_{ij} = \left[\sum_{q=1}^{p} (x_{jq} - x_{iq})^2 \right]^{1/2} = \left[\sum_{q=1}^{p} (x_{jq}^2 - 2x_{jq}x_{iq} + x_{iq}^2) \right]^{1/2}$$

$$= \left[\sum_{q=1}^{p} x_{jq}^2 + \sum_{q=1}^{p} x_{iq}^2 - 2 \sum_{q=1}^{p} x_{jq}x_{iq} \right]^{1/2}$$

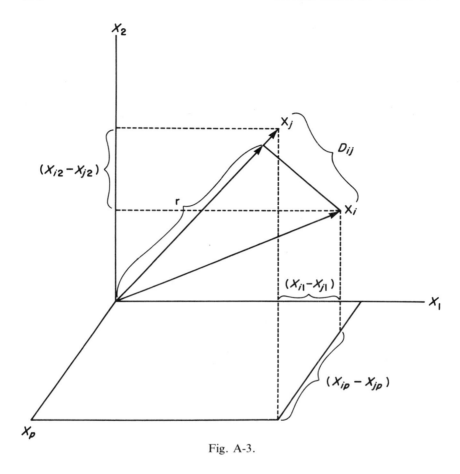

Fig. A-3.

This expansion indicates that D_{ij} is diminished as the vector product increases. In the case of orthogonal vectors, D_{ij} becomes a function of the squared norms of the two vectors as the vector product is zero: in fact, since D_{ij} becomes the square root of the sum of the two norms squared, it can be thought of as the hypotenuse of a right-angled triangle, with the vectors forming the two sides.

Appendix B
Some Basic Matrix Calculations

A matrix can be viewed as a series of vectors arranged in rows or columns. The resulting number of rows of the matrix and the resulting number of columns define its order. Matrices are usually represented with upper-case, boldface letters. For example, a matrix with p rows and N columns is designated as a p by N matrix, $\mathbf{A}$ (the number of rows precede the number of columns in the order designation). Matrix $\mathbf{A}$ could represent the scores on p measures for each of N subjects; in this case, a given row designated q (where $q = 1, 2, \ldots, p$) corresponds to the scores across the N subjects for measure q and a given column, i (where $i = 1, 2, \ldots, N$) corresponds to the profile of scores on the p measures for subject i. If the number of rows in a matrix is equal to the number of columns, the matrix is said to be square.

The individual values in a matrix are called its elements. They are typically denoted by the lower case of the letter designating the matrix with subscripts referring to the row and column in which they are located, in that order. For matrix $\mathbf{A}$, the element in the qth row and i^{th} column is denoted a_{qi}. Hence, matrix $\mathbf{A}$ is represented as the following array of values:

$$\mathbf{A} = \begin{pmatrix} a_{11} & a_{12} & a_{13} & \cdots & a_{1i} & \cdots & a_{1N} \\ a_{21} & a_{22} & a_{23} & \cdots & a_{2i} & \cdots & a_{2N} \\ a_{31} & a_{32} & a_{33} & \cdots & a_{3i} & \cdots & a_{3N} \\ \cdot & \cdot & \cdot & \cdots & \cdot & \cdots & \cdot \\ a_{q1} & a_{q2} & a_{q3} & \cdots & a_{qi} & \cdots & a_{qN} \\ \cdot & \cdot & \cdot & \cdots & \cdot & \cdots & \cdot \\ a_{p1} & a_{p2} & a_{p3} & \cdots & a_{pi} & \cdots & a_{pN} \end{pmatrix}$$

Two matrices of the same order, a p by N matrix $\mathbf{A}$ and a p by N matrix $\mathbf{B}$, may be summed by adding their corresponding elements ($a_{qi} + b_{qi}$) to form the matrix sum $\mathbf{A} + \mathbf{B}$. Subtraction of equal-order matrices proceeds in a similar manner, but with the differences rather than the sums of the corresponding elements. Addition and subtraction of matrices is simply an extension of addition and subtraction of vectors; it can be thought of as adding or subtracting corresponding column vectors.

The transpose of a matrix is obtained when its column vectors are arranged into rows and its row vectors become its columns. The transpose is usually denoted with a prime following the matrix designation. For example, the transpose of $\mathbf{A}$ would be:

$$\mathbf{A}' = \begin{pmatrix} a_{11} & a_{21} & a_{31} & \cdots & a_{q1} & \cdots & a_{p1} \\ a_{12} & a_{22} & a_{32} & \cdots & a_{q2} & \cdots & a_{p2} \\ a_{13} & a_{23} & a_{33} & \cdots & a_{q3} & \cdots & a_{p3} \\ \cdot & \cdot & \cdot & \cdots & \cdot & \cdots & \cdot \\ a_{1i} & a_{2i} & a_{3i} & \cdots & a_{qi} & \cdots & a_{pi} \\ \cdot & \cdot & \cdot & \cdots & \cdot & \cdots & \cdot \\ a_{1N} & a_{2N} & a_{3N} & \cdots & a_{qN} & \cdots & a_{pN} \end{pmatrix}$$

The order of $\mathbf{A}'$ is N by p, the opposite of the order of $\mathbf{A}$.

A *symmetric* matrix is a square matrix (one with equal numbers of rows and columns) with special properties. The elements with identical subscripts designating row and column locations, e.g., a_{11}, a_{22}, a_{33}, . . . , a_{pp} (where $\mathbf{A}$ is a p by p matrix), are referred to as the diagonal elements. In a symmetric matrix, the configuration of elements above the diagonals are a reflection of those below the diagonals. An example of a symmetric matrix is:

$$\begin{pmatrix} 2 & 1 & 3 & 7 \\ 1 & 4 & 6 & 2 \\ 3 & 6 & 6 & 5 \\ 7 & 2 & 5 & 8 \end{pmatrix}$$

In this case, a_{ij} is equal to a_{ji} (where $i, j = 1, 2, \ldots, p$; $i \neq j$). The element a_{12} would be equal to the element with subscripts reversed, a_{21}; a_{13} would equal a_{31}, a_{24} would equal a_{42}, and so on. Note that in this case, the rows and columns are identical so that $\mathbf{A} = \mathbf{A}'$. Symmetric matrices are often used in statistical analyses because the entity designating a given column is the same as the entity designating the row with the equivalent column value.

To illustrate, consider the p by N matrix $\mathbf{A}$ used before. Suppose again that the column vectors represent the profiles of scores on the p measures for the respective N subjects. The investigator wishes to obtain the vector products among the columns for the N subjects. He obtains the vector product between subjects one and two by multiplying the vector corresponding to the first column by that corresponding to the second column. The vector product between subjects one and three are likewise obtained as the vector product between columns one and three, and so on. Each of these values represents the relationship in vector-product form between the corresponding pair of subjects; the vector product represents the length of projection of one subject vector onto the other times the norm of the other's vector (see Appendix A). These vector products are then arranged into an N by N matrix of vector products. Column j, as well as the row with the corresponding number to the column, represents the vector products between subject j and the remaining $(N - 1)$ subjects. Hence, the matrix is symmetric since the rows and columns are interchangeable and element a_{ij} is equal to element a_{ji}. It is clear that the vector product between any two subjects, such as 2 and 3, is the same as the vector product between subjects 3 and 2 since, in each case, the same values have been entered into the vector–product computation.

A symmetric matrix of order p by p may also be formed from the vector products among the rows of the p by N matrix, $\mathbf{A}$. In this case, the elements indicate the relations among the p measures in the sense that each vector product represents the length of the projection of one measure onto the other times the norm of the other's vector. Again, the matrix is symmetric.

A type of matrix often encountered in multivariate analyses is a p by p correlation matrix. The elements of a correlation matrix can be thought of as a matrix of the vector products among the rows of the p by N matrix. However, before obtaining the vector products, the mean of the N scores in a given row q is first subtracted from each of the row's values. Next, the resulting differences are divided by the value $N^{1/2}\sigma_q$, where σ_q is the standard deviation of the measure calculated over the row's N subjects. Consequently, element $r_{qq'}$ (where $q, q' = 1, 2, \ldots, p$) of a p by p correlation matrix $\mathbf{R}$ is equal to:

$$\sum_{i=1}^{N} (a_{qi} - \bar{a}_q.)(a_{q'i} - \bar{a}_{q'}.)/N\sigma_q\sigma_{q'}$$

MATRIX MULTIPLICATION

A p by N matrix can be multiplied by an N by z matrix by obtaining the vector products between the row vectors of the first matrix and the column vectors of the second matrix. Let the first matrix be $\mathbf{A}$ and the second be $\mathbf{B}$. The product is written as $\mathbf{AB}$ and the resulting matrix product is denoted $\mathbf{C}$. Written in this way, $\mathbf{A}$ is said to be post-multiplied by $\mathbf{B}$, or $\mathbf{B}$ premultiplied by $\mathbf{A}$, to give $\mathbf{C}$. To carry out multiplication, the number of columns in the first matrix must be equal to the number of rows in the second. The element c_{qf} of matrix $\mathbf{C}$ is the vector product between row q of matrix $\mathbf{A}$ and column f of matrix $\mathbf{B}$:

$$\sum_{i=1}^{N} a_{qi}b_{if} \text{ (where } q = 1, 2, \ldots, p; f = 1, 2, \ldots, z)$$

The order of the product corresponds to the number of rows in the first matrix and the number of columns in the second matrix. Thus, $\mathbf{C}$ is of the order p by z. For example, consider the following matrices $\mathbf{A}$ and $\mathbf{B}$, and their product $\mathbf{C}$:

$$\mathbf{A} = \begin{pmatrix} 1 & 3 & 4 & 2 \\ 3 & 6 & 1 & 5 \\ 2 & 8 & 7 & 4 \end{pmatrix} \quad \mathbf{B} = \begin{pmatrix} 2 & 4 \\ 6 & 3 \\ 7 & 8 \\ 5 & 1 \end{pmatrix}$$

$$\mathbf{C} = \begin{pmatrix} 58 & 47 \\ 74 & 43 \\ 121 & 92 \end{pmatrix}$$

e.g. $c_{11} = (1)(2) + (3)(6) + (4)(7) + (2)(5) = 58$.

It is helpful to conceptualize matrix multiplication as taking a matrix whose elements refer to one set of referent axes and transforming it onto another set of referent axes. For example, in a p by N

matrix $\mathbf{A}$, the p rows can be thought of as p vectors, each coordinate referring to one of N referent axes. The matrix by which $\mathbf{A}$ is post-multiplied is an $\mathbf{N}$ by z matrix $\mathbf{B}$, which has N row vectors, each with z coordinates referring to z referent axes. Let the $\mathbf{N}$ referent axes of $\mathbf{A}$ be denoted x_i (where $i = 1, 2, \ldots, N$) and the z referent axes of $\mathbf{B}$ as w_f (where $f = 1, 2, \ldots, z$). In addition, let the p row vectors of $\mathbf{A}$ be written as p linear relations:

$$\mathbf{a}_1 = a_{11}x_1 + a_{12}x_2 + \cdots + a_{1N}x_N$$
$$\mathbf{a}_2 = a_{21}x_1 + a_{22}x_2 + \cdots + a_{2N}x_N$$
$$\cdot \qquad \cdot \qquad \cdot \qquad \cdots \qquad \cdot$$
$$\mathbf{a}_p = a_{p1}x_1 + a_{p2}x_2 + \cdots + a_{pN}x_N$$

Let the row vectors of $\mathbf{B}$ be written as N linear relations:

$$\mathbf{x}_1 = b_{11}w_1 + b_{12}w_2 + \cdots + b_{1z}w_z$$
$$\mathbf{x}_2 = b_{21}w_1 + b_{22}w_2 + \cdots + b_{2z}w_z$$
$$\cdot \qquad \cdot \qquad \cdot \qquad \cdots \qquad \cdot$$
$$\mathbf{x}_N = b_{N1}w_1 + b_{N2}w_2 + \cdots + b_{Nz}w_z$$

It is apparent from the preceding sets of linear relations that the coordinates of $\mathbf{B}$'s row vectors have been used to designate the relationship of the referent axes x_i of $\mathbf{A}$ to the referent axes w_f of $\mathbf{B}$. By knowing the relationship of the row vectors in $\mathbf{A}$ to the N reference axes (the coordinates of these row vectors), and by knowing the relationship of the reference axes x_i to the alternate reference axes w_f, we calculate the relationship of the row vectors of $\mathbf{A}$ to the reference axes w_f. We replace the x_is with their w_f coordinates, using the row vectors of $\mathbf{B}$. The row vectors of $\mathbf{A}$ become:

$$\mathbf{a}_1 = a_{11}(b_{11}w_1 + b_{12}w_2 + \cdots + b_{1z}w_z)$$
$$+ a_{12}(b_{21}w_1 + b_{22}w_2 + \cdots + b_{2z}w_z)$$
$$+ \cdots + a_{1N}(b_{N1}w_1 + b_{N2}w_2 + \cdots + b_{Nz}w_z)$$
$$\mathbf{a}_2 = a_{21}(b_{11}w_1 + b_{12}w_2 + \cdots + b_{1z}w_z)$$
$$+ a_{22}(b_{21}w_1 + b_{22}w_2 + \cdots + b_{2z}w_z)$$
$$+ \cdots + a_{2N}(b_{N1}w_1 + b_{N2}w_2 + \cdots + b_{Nz}w_z)$$
$$\cdot \qquad \cdot \qquad \cdot \qquad \cdot$$
$$\mathbf{a}_p = a_{p1}(b_{11}w_1 + b_{12}w_2 + \cdots + b_{1z}w_z)$$
$$+ a_{p2}(b_{21}w_1 + b_{22}w_2 + \cdots + b_{2z}w_z)$$
$$+ \cdots + a_{pN}(b_{N1}w_1 + b_{N2}w_2 + \cdots + b_{Nz}w_z).$$

By rearranging these linear relations, it is possible to define the respective $\mathbf{a}_q$ in terms of coordinates relevant to the z referents, w_f:

$$
\begin{aligned}
\mathbf{a}_1 = &(a_{11}b_{11} + a_{12}b_{21} + \cdots + a_{1N}b_{N1})w_1 \\
&+ (a_{11}b_{12} + a_{12}b_{22} + \cdots + a_{1N}b_{N2})w_2 \\
&+ \cdots + (a_{11}b_{1z} + a_{12}b_{2z} + \cdots + a_{1N}b_{Nz})w_z \\
\mathbf{a}_2 = &(a_{21}b_{11} + a_{22}b_{21} + \cdots + a_{2N}b_{N1})w_1 \\
&+ (a_{21}b_{12} + a_{22}b_{22} + \cdots + a_{2N}b_{N2})w_2 \\
&+ \cdots + (a_{21}b_{1z} + a_{22}b_{2z} + \cdots + a_{2N}b_{Nz})w_z \\
& \qquad \cdot \qquad \cdot \qquad \cdot \qquad \cdot \\
\mathbf{a}_p = &(a_{p1}b_{11} + a_{p2}b_{21} + \cdots + a_{pN}b_{N1})w_1 \\
&+ (a_{p1}b_{12} + a_{p2}b_{22} + \cdots + a_{pN}b_{N2})w_2 \\
&+ \cdots + (a_{p1}b_{1z} + a_{p2}b_{2z} + \cdots + a_{pN}b_{Nz})w_z
\end{aligned}
$$

Note that the bracketed terms preceding the respective w_fs represent the elements of the matrix product $\mathbf{C}$. Thus, $\mathbf{C}$ represents the matrix $\mathbf{A}$ transformed according to its w_f coordinates by using the coefficients in the matrix $\mathbf{B}$. We can examine the set of linear relations to ascertain that the vectors $\mathbf{a}_q$ are transformed by weighting their relationships to the respective x_i axes (their coordinates, a_{qi}) according to the relationships of the x_i axes to the w_f axes (the coordinates of the x_i axes with respect to the w_f axes, represented by the elements in $\mathbf{B}$).

As a final note, we mention that a nonsquare matrix is used to form a square matrix by pre- or post-multiplying it by its transpose. For a p by N matrix $\mathbf{A}$, the product $\mathbf{A}'\mathbf{A}$ is an N by N matrix, and the product $\mathbf{AA}'$ is a p by p matrix.

THE DETERMINANT OF A MATRIX

An important property of a matrix in much statistical analysis is its determinant. Before computing to find the determinant of any matrix of order p by p, we should consider the determinant of a 2 by 2 matrix. The 2 by 2 matrix $\mathbf{A}$ would appear as:

$$
\mathbf{A} = \begin{pmatrix} a_{11} & a_{12} \\ a_{21} & a_{22} \end{pmatrix}
$$

The determinant of $\mathbf{A}$, notated as $|\mathbf{A}|$, is obtained as the product of the elements on the diagonals minus the product of the elements on the off-diagonals, $(a_{11}a_{22}) - (a_{21}a_{12})$. The *cofactor* of an element a_{ij}— where $i, j = 1, 2, \ldots , p$; in the present example, p being 2—is $(-1)^{i+j}$ times the determinant obtained from the $(p - ,1)$ by $(p - 1)$ matrix that results from deletion of the row and column of the element a_{ij}. In the case of the 2 by 2 matrix, the cofactor of a_{ij} is the element remaining after row i and j have been deleted, times $(-1)^{i+j}$. The determinant is obtained by first taking any row or column of the p by p matrix and successively finding the cofactors of the elements in the row or column. The elements are then multiplied by their cofactors and the products summed to give the determinant. In our example of the 2 by 2 matrix, we have selected the first column of elements. The element a_{22} is the determinant of the one-element residual $(p - 1)$ by $(p - 1)$ matrix resulting from deletion of the first row and first column of the original matrix. Therefore, the cofactor of a_{11} is $(-1)^{1+1}a_{22}$. The cofactor is multiplied by the corresponding element a_{11}. Similarly, the cofactor of a_{21} is $(-1)^{1+2}a_{12}$, which is multiplied by its corresponding element a_{21}. The sum of the products is the determinant of the 2 by 2 matrix.

This procedure can be extended to a 3 by 3 matrix. In this case, a row or column of the matrix is selected and the elements are multiplied by their cofactors and summed. Consider the following matrix and its determinant:

$$\mathbf{A} = \begin{pmatrix} a_{11} & a_{12} & a_{13} \\ a_{21} & a_{22} & a_{23} \\ a_{31} & a_{32} & a_{33} \end{pmatrix}$$

Selecting the first column,

$$|\mathbf{A}| = a_{11} \begin{vmatrix} 22 & 23 \\ a_{32} & a_{33} \end{vmatrix} - a_{21} \begin{vmatrix} 12 & 13 \\ a_{32} & a_{33} \end{vmatrix} + a_{31} \begin{vmatrix} 12 & 13 \\ a_{22} & a_{23} \end{vmatrix}$$
$$= a_{11}(a_{22}a_{33} - a_{32}a_{23}) - a_{21}(a_{12}a_{33} - a_{32}a_{13}) + a_{31}(a_{12}a_{23} - a_{22}a_{13})$$

In the case of a 4 by 4 matrix, the calculation of cofactors for the four elements of any row or column is again required, followed by multiplication with their corresponding elements, and the products then summed. The cofactors require the computation of four determinants of four 3 by 3 matrices which are obtained by successively deleting the rows and columns of the respective elements in the selected row or column. Calculation of these cofactors—the determinants of the 3 by 3 matrices times $(-1)^{i+j}$—would proceed as in the former example. Calculation of the determinant of a 5 by 5 matrix requires the computation of the determinants of five 4 by 4 matrices, and so on.

In general, the determinant of a p by p matrix requires the computation of p determinants of p matrices, each of order $(p-1)$ by $(p-1)$. Each cofactor is multiplied by $(-1)^{i+j}$ as well as by the corresponding element. Finally, the products are summed. Once the rules of computation are understood, calculation of the determinant of any square matrix can be undertaken in this fashion. Of course, the computational labor for even a moderately sized matrix is overwhelming and requires the use of an appropriate computer program. Computer packages for quantitative methods requiring matrix determinants typically include these computations as subroutines. Several of these packaged programs are cited throughout this book.

Inverse of a Matrix

When the determinant of a matrix has been found, obtaining the inverse is quite straightforward. The first requirement is to obtain the cofactor of every element in the matrix. The cofactor of element a_{ij} is denoted A_{ij}. The cofactors are arranged into a matrix, with each element located in the row and column of the element to which it corresponds; that is, A_{ij} would be in column i and row j of the matrix of cofactors. The matrix of cofactors for matrix $\mathbf{A}$ is called the *adjoint* of $\mathbf{A}$. If we take the transpose of the adjoint and divide each element by the determinant of $\mathbf{A}$, we have the inverse of $\mathbf{A}$ denoted as $\mathbf{A}^{-1}$.

The inverse of a matrix is analogous to the inverse of a single number. A number divided by itself is equal to one. A matrix multiplied by its inverse is equal to a matrix with ones on its diagonals and zeros on its off-diagonals. Such a matrix is called an identity matrix, denoted $\mathbf{I}$. Just as a number multiplied by one equals the original number, a matrix multiplied by the identity matrix equals the original matrix.

Consider this example of a 3 by 3 matrix and the computations of its inverse:

$$\mathbf{A} = \begin{pmatrix} 1 & 3 & 2 \\ 1 & 1 & 2 \\ 2 & 1 & 3 \end{pmatrix} \qquad |\mathbf{A}| = 2$$

$$\text{Adjoint of } \mathbf{A} = \begin{pmatrix} 1 & 1 & -1 \\ -7 & -1 & 5 \\ 4 & 0 & -2 \end{pmatrix}$$

$$\text{Transpose of adjoint of } \mathbf{A} = \begin{pmatrix} 1 & -7 & 4 \\ 1 & -1 & 0 \\ -1 & -5 & -2 \end{pmatrix}$$

$$\mathbf{A}^{-1} = \begin{pmatrix} \frac{1}{2} & -7/2 & 4/2 \\ \frac{1}{2} & -\frac{1}{2} & 0 \\ -\frac{1}{2} & 5/2 & -2/2 \end{pmatrix} = \begin{pmatrix} .5 & -3.5 & 2 \\ .5 & -.5 & 0 \\ -.5 & 2.5 & -1 \end{pmatrix}$$

$$\mathbf{A}\mathbf{A}^{-1} = \begin{pmatrix} 1 & 3 & 2 \\ 1 & 1 & 2 \\ 2 & 1 & 3 \end{pmatrix} \begin{pmatrix} .5 & -3.5 & 2 \\ .5 & -.5 & 0 \\ -.5 & 2.5 & -1 \end{pmatrix} = \begin{pmatrix} 1 & 0 & 0 \\ 0 & 1 & 0 \\ 0 & 0 & 1 \end{pmatrix} = \mathbf{I}$$

LATENT ROOTS AND LATENT VECTORS

A vital part of most multivariate statistical procedures involves the use of the latent roots and latent vectors of a matrix. These vectors represent the essence of a matrix in that they can be used to reproduce it. In addition, the latent roots correspond the relative importance of the latent vectors in reproducing the matrix. The matrices discussed in this book are called *positive semidefinite*, meaning that they have no negative latent roots. However, they may have latent roots that are zero or nearly zero. The contribution to matrix reproduction of the latent vectors corresponding to these small latent roots is negligable, and not usually retained for serious consideration.

Inasmuch as the latent vectors can be used to reproduce the matrix from which they were derived, they can also be used to ascertain the nature of the data configuration in the original matrix. In addition, they provide parsimony in describing the nature of the original matrix: A p by p matrix can have p column or p row vectors, and p latent roots. If a number of the latent roots are zero or near zero, their corresponding latent vectors are disregarded. Consequently, the number of vectors to be taken into account is reduced from p to p minus the number of negligeably sized latent roots. In practice, only the latent vectors of substantially large latent roots are retained for examination. In some cases the statistical significance of the size of the latent roots and vectors can be tested, and the only latent vectors retained for further consideration will be those whose sets of elements are not likely to have been produced by random sources of variation. In order to determine the values of the latent roots (the fth latent root denoted λ_f), the matrix must first have the unknown λ subtracted from its diagonals. The equation for the determinant of the resulting matrix is then constructed and set equal to zero. The equation will be of the form:

$$(-\lambda)^p + c_{p-1}(-\lambda)^{p-1} + c_{p-2}(-\lambda)^{p-2} + \cdots - c_1\lambda + |\mathbf{A}| = 0$$

There are potentially p different nonzero values for λ that will satisfy this equation. For a positive semidefinite matrix none of these values will be negative.

The latent vectors of the latent roots are obtained in the following way. The value of the latent root λ_f is subtracted from the diagonals of the matrix. A vector $\mathbf{x}_f$ is then constructed with p coordinates such that all the vector products between each row of the matrix and $\mathbf{x}_f$ are equal to zero. If our matrix were a p by p matrix $\mathbf{A}$, this requirement would be written as $(\mathbf{A} - \lambda_f\mathbf{I})\mathbf{x}_f = \mathbf{0}$. Here, $\lambda_f\mathbf{I}$ is a p by p matrix with λ_f for each of its diagonal elements and zeros as the off-diagonals. The term $\mathbf{0}$ denotes a p-tuple vector whose coordinates are all zero.

In the following 2 by 2 matrix we compute the latent roots and latent vectors. Note that since neither root is equal to zero, the number of latent vectors is equal to the number of row or column vectors in the original matrix:

$$\mathbf{A} = \begin{pmatrix} 10 & 5 \\ 5 & 8 \end{pmatrix} \quad \mathbf{A} - \lambda\mathbf{I} = \begin{pmatrix} 10 - \lambda & 5 \\ 5 & 8 - \lambda \end{pmatrix}$$

$$|\mathbf{A} - \lambda\mathbf{I}| = (10 - \lambda)(8 - \lambda) - 25 = \lambda^2 - 18\lambda + 55$$

Setting the determinantal equation equal to zero, we have:

$$\lambda^2 - 18\lambda + 55 = 0$$

Values of λ satisfying this equation are 14.1 and 3.9. Thus $\lambda_1 = 14.1$ and $\lambda_2 = 3.9$. We obtain $\mathbf{x}_1$ as the vector satisfying:

$$(\mathbf{A} - \lambda_1\mathbf{I})\mathbf{x}_1 = \mathbf{0}$$

$$\begin{pmatrix} -4.1 & 5 \\ 5 & -6.1 \end{pmatrix} \begin{pmatrix} 2 \\ 1.64 \end{pmatrix} = \begin{pmatrix} 0 \\ 0 \end{pmatrix}$$

Thus $\mathbf{x}_1 = \begin{pmatrix} 2 \\ 1.64 \end{pmatrix}$. Via similar procedures, we obtain $\mathbf{x}_2$ as $\begin{pmatrix} -1.64 \\ 2 \end{pmatrix}$

A p by p matrix can be reproduced from its latent vectors by carrying out the following operations. Each latent vector is taken in turn and its coordinates multiplied by the square root of the corresponding latent root times the reciprocal of the norm of the latent vector. This procedure is known as normalizing the latent vector to its latent root. The norm of each resulting vector will then be equal to the square root of the corresponding latent root. The latent vectors normalized in this way can be arranged in columns to form a p by m matrix $\mathbf{P}$, where m is the number of nonzero latent roots. If this matrix is post-multiplied by its transpose, the product will be the original matrix $\mathbf{A}$. Furthermore, if $\mathbf{P}$ is premultiplied by its transpose, the product will be a matrix with the latent roots as the diagonal elements and zeros as the off-diagonal elements. To illustrate, we return to the latent vectors of our previous 2 by 2 matrix, $\mathbf{A}$:

$$(\lambda_1^{1/2})/(\mathbf{x}_1'\mathbf{x}_1)^{1/2} = 1.45$$

$$1.45\mathbf{x}_1 = \begin{pmatrix} 2.90 \\ 2.38 \end{pmatrix}$$

$$(\lambda_2^{1/2})/(\mathbf{x}_2'\mathbf{x}_2)^{1/2}\mathbf{x}_2 = \begin{pmatrix} -1.25 \\ 1.52 \end{pmatrix}$$

$$\mathbf{P} = \begin{pmatrix} 2.90 & -1.25 \\ 2.38 & 1.52 \end{pmatrix}$$

$$\mathbf{A} = \mathbf{P}\mathbf{P}' = \begin{pmatrix} 2.90 & -1.25 \\ 2.38 & 1.52 \end{pmatrix} \begin{pmatrix} 2.90 & 2.38 \\ -1.25 & 1.52 \end{pmatrix} = \begin{pmatrix} 10 & 5 \\ 5 & 8 \end{pmatrix}$$

$$\mathbf{P}'\mathbf{P} = \begin{pmatrix} 14.1 & 0 \\ 0 & 3.9 \end{pmatrix}$$

We can examine these operations to ascertain that when the norms of the latent vectors are originally equal or have been normalized to one (see Appendix A), their respective contributions to the reconstruction of the original matrix varies with the size of their corresponding latent roots. Where a latent root is zero or very small, the contribution of its latent vector is also zero or negligeable. For that reason, it is customary to use the size of a latent root as an index of how much weight to place on the inferences drawn about a matrix from the coordinates of a latent vector.

One final property of latent vectors should be noted. The vector product between any two latent vectors is zero. Thus, latent vectors are orthogonal to one another, meaning that the length of one projection onto another is zero (see Appendix A).

Appendix C
Iterative Computation of Latent Roots and Latent Vectors

The following procedure for computing latent roots and latent vectors was presented by Van de Geer.[1] It can be carried out with a desk calculator for square matrices provided that their order is not very large.

Let the matrix be a p by p matrix, $\mathbf{A}$. A p-tuple vector $\mathbf{b}_{12}$ is obtained by post-multiplying $\mathbf{A}$ by a p-tuple vector $\mathbf{b}_{11}$, whose elements are all one. Therefore $\mathbf{b}_{12}$ will equal the row totals of $\mathbf{A}$. Each coordinate of $\mathbf{b}_{12}$ is divided by its largest element to give $\mathbf{b}_{13}$. The product $\mathbf{Ab}_{13}$ is obtained and, after dividing it by its largest coordinate, we have $\mathbf{b}_{14}$. For example, consider the a 3 by 3 matrix:

$$\mathbf{A} = \begin{pmatrix} 3 & 2 & 1 \\ 2 & 2 & 4 \\ 1 & 4 & 2 \end{pmatrix}$$

$$\mathbf{b}_{12} = \mathbf{Ab}_{11} = \begin{pmatrix} 3 & 2 & 1 \\ 2 & 2 & 4 \\ 1 & 4 & 2 \end{pmatrix} \begin{pmatrix} 1 \\ 1 \\ 1 \end{pmatrix} = \begin{pmatrix} 6 \\ 8 \\ 7 \end{pmatrix}$$

$$\mathbf{b}_{13} = \tfrac{1}{8}\mathbf{b}_{12} = \begin{pmatrix} .75 \\ 1 \\ .875 \end{pmatrix}$$

The vector $\mathbf{b}_{14}$ is then obtained as the vector resulting from $\mathbf{Ab}_{13}$ divided by its largest coordinate. The vector $\mathbf{b}_{15}$ is obtained in a similar manner—$\mathbf{Ab}_{14}$ divided by its largest coordinate. This process is continued until a vector $\mathbf{Ab}_{1h}$ is obtained which again yields $\mathbf{b}_{1h}$ when divided by its largest coordinate. When the vectors converge in this way, their coordinates are those of the first latent vector, and the largest element of $\mathbf{Ab}_{1h}$ is equal to the first latent root.

In applying this procedure to matrix $\mathbf{A}$ of our example, we continue until we obtain $\mathbf{b}_{19}$:

$$\mathbf{b}_{19} = \begin{pmatrix} .71099 \\ 1 \\ .9219 \end{pmatrix}$$

$$\mathbf{Ab}_{19} = \begin{pmatrix} 5.0549 \\ 7.1096 \\ 6.5548 \end{pmatrix}$$

$$\mathbf{b}_{1,10} = (1/7.1096)\mathbf{Ab}_{19} = \begin{pmatrix} .71099 \\ 1 \\ .9219 \end{pmatrix}$$

The first latent root is 7.1096.

To find the second latent root and vector, we apply the same procedure to the residual matrix $\mathbf{A}_1$. To obtain $\mathbf{A}_1$, we subtract from $\mathbf{A}$ a matrix reconstructed from the first latent vector of $\mathbf{A}$. To reconstruct the matrix from the first latent vector, $\mathbf{b}_{1h}$, we first normalize the vector to the first latent root. Let $\mathbf{b}_{1h}$, so normalized, be denoted $\mathbf{f}_{1h}$. The reconstructed matrix subtracted from $\mathbf{A}$ to give $\mathbf{A}_1$, is obtained as $\mathbf{f}_{1h}\mathbf{f}'_{1h}$. Returning to our example, we obtain $\mathbf{f}_{19}$ as:

$$\mathbf{f}_{19} = (7.1096)^{1/2}/(2.355)^{1/2}\mathbf{b}_{19}$$

$$= 1.7375\mathbf{b}_{19} = \begin{pmatrix} 1.2353 \\ 1.7375 \\ 1.6018 \end{pmatrix}$$

$$\mathbf{f}_{19}\mathbf{f}'_{19} = \begin{pmatrix} 1.2353 \\ 1.7375 \\ 1.6018 \end{pmatrix} \cdot (1.2353, 1.7375, 1.6018)$$

$$= \begin{pmatrix} 1.5260 & 2.1463 & 1.9787 \\ 2.1463 & 3.0189 & 2.7831 \\ 1.9787 & 2.7831 & 2.5658 \end{pmatrix}$$

$$\mathbf{A}_1 = \mathbf{A} - (\mathbf{f}_{19}\mathbf{f}'_{19}) = \begin{pmatrix} 1.474 & -.1463 & -.9787 \\ -.1463 & -1.0189 & 1.2169 \\ -.9787 & 1.2169 & -.5658 \end{pmatrix}$$

We continue the procedure applied to A_1 until finding the second latent vector b_{2h}, whose coordinates are equal to $b_{2,h+1}$. The largest coordinate of $A_1 b_h$ is the second latent root. A second residual matrix A_2 is found by subtracting $f_{2h} f'_{2h}$ from A_1; where f_{2h} is equal to b_{2h} normalized to the second latent root. The process is then applied to A_2 to find the third latent root and latent vector. This final operation exhausts all the latent roots and latent vectors of a 3 by 3 matrix. For matrices of larger order, the procedure is iterated further until all the latent roots and latent vectors have been obtained, or until the changes in the elements of two successive residual matrices are of negligible size.

Van de Geer pointed out that convergence to the latent roots and vectors is accelerated if rows and columns of a residual matrix having many negative values are each multiplied by (-1). In so doing, the corresponding coordinates of the obtained latent vector must be multiplied by (-1). For example, if the last two rows and columns of A_1 were multiplied by (-1), the last two coordinates of b_{2h} would also be multiplied by (-1).

Another method of expediting convergence of vectors is to apply the procedure after multiplying A by itself one or more times. For example, $A^2 = AA$; $A^3 = (AA)A$; and so on. In this case, the latent vectors do not change, but the largest coordinate of the vector obtained as A raised to the xth power post-multiplied by the latent vector, is equal to the latent root of A also raised to the xth power. That is, if the procedure were applied to A^3, the largest coordinate of $A^3 b_{1h}$ would be equal to the first latent root of A, cubed.

REFERENCE

1. Van de Geer, J. P. Introduction to multivariate analysis for the social sciences. San Francisco: Freeman, 1971, p. 273.

Index

Page numbers in italics refer to figures; page numbers followed by t refer to tables.

Randall Library – UNCW

RC337 .N47   NXWW
Neufeld / Clinical quantitative methods

304900240722X